BIOLOGY
Experiments
for Children

Formerly titled BIOLOGY FOR CHILDREN

Written and Illustrated by
Ethel Hanauer

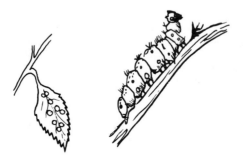

Dover Publications, Inc., New York

Published in Canada by General Publishing Company, Ltd.,
30 Lesmill Road, Don Mills, Toronto, Ontario.

Published in the United Kingdom by Constable and Company, Ltd.,
10 Orange Street, London WC 2.

This Dover edition, first published in 1968, is an unabridged
and unaltered republication of the work originally published in
1962 under the title *Biology for Children*. The work is reprinted
by special arrangement with Printed Arts Company, Inc., pub-
lisher of the original edition.

Standard Book Number: 486-22032-X
Library of Congress Catalog Card Number: 68-9305

Manufactured in the United States of America

Dover Publications, Inc.
180 Varick Street
New York, N. Y. 10014

CONTENTS

To Richard and Billy
for their help, patience and understanding

Part I: THE NATURE OF ALL LIVING THINGS

When you think of "living things," you probably think first of the animals and people you are most familiar with. You might think of your pets—a dog, a cat, a hamster, a canary, a tank of tropical fish—or of the animals in the zoo, or of human animals, your parents and friends. Think about it some more, and you will realize that plants are living, too. You might think of your favorite tree for climbing, of the leaves you gather during fall, or perhaps of the crocuses and snow drops which everyone is so glad to see pushing through the snow in early spring.

Remember, too, that many of the inert, lifeless things you use every day originally had life. The wood in your desk came from a tree, as did the paper on which this book is printed. Threads for a pure silk tie or dress were spun by the caterpillars of silk moths. The wool in your winter coat once kept a sheep warm. The coal we burn to provide heat had its origin in giant fern trees which existed millions of years ago, and then disappeared from the earth as its climate changed.

These are the living things which come most readily to mind. But there are thousands of other living organisms on the earth—in the air and in the water. Look into a jar of water which you have taken from a pond. You will see tiny water animals darting about, but there are others there, too, that are much too small to be visible to your "naked," or unaided eye. To see them you will need a microscope. With its help, you will be able to watch minute, unsuspected animals scooting through the water or oozing lazily along, according to their nature. You will also be able to see the tiny plants that serve as food for these microscopic animals.

Equipment you will need

For your study of living things you will need a microscope. Good ones are available at inexpensive prices. Your microscope will last for a very long time if you take good care of it. It will be your basic tool, the most important aid in your exploration of the nature of life. With its help you will be able to see the simplest structures of which all life is composed, cells and tissues. Your microscope will open to you new worlds of life and exciting experiences observing living things both visible and invisible to your naked eye.

In addition, you will want to buy several glass slides and one or more cover slips, little round disks of glass or plastic which you will place over the tiny objects you will be examining under your microscope.

The object on a slide is called a "specimen." As for your specimens, most of them are easy to find. They are all around you. You need only walk around your house, into your yard or to the neighborhood stores to gather the specimens you will study.

Now, you are ready to begin your fascinating explorations.

USING YOUR MICROSCOPE

Before you begin your venture into the world of living things, you will need one important skill; you will need to know how to operate your microscope quickly and correctly.

No matter how inexpensive, a compound microscope usually looks like the one shown in the illustration below.

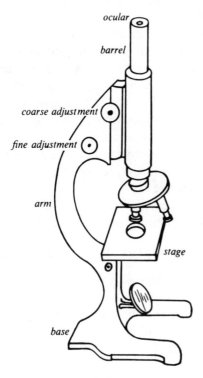

Learn the important parts of the microscope and the use of each part before you try to view something that is almost or completely invisible to your naked eye. It is a good idea to refer to the illustration as you read these instructions.

Always carry your microscope upright by holding the *arm* with one hand and supporting its weight under the *base* with your other hand. Set it down gently on a firm table top near a window, if possible. If that is not possible, use it near an electric light.

When you are ready to operate your microscope, align (get into a straight line) the low power objective with the tube. When it's aligned, you'll hear it click into place.

Now move the curved side of the mirror until it catches the light and directs it up into the tube, through the eyepiece or *ocular* into your eye.

Place your prepared slide in the center of the *stage* over the hole. As you watch the shorter, low power objective, turn the larger wheel, or *coarse adjustment*, until it is about a quarter of an inch away from the slide on the stage.

Put your eye to the ocular. Slowly raise the tube, or *barrel*, by turning the coarse adjustment toward you. The specimen on the slide will gradually come into clear view or *focus*.

When the specimen is focused, switch to the *fine adjustment*. Keep your eye at the eyepiece. Turn the small wheel, or fine adjustment, very slowly until the magnified specimen comes into view with increasing clearness.

The lens in the eyepiece, or *ocular*, of most microscopes will magnify an object ten times. The lens in the low power objective will magnify ten times, also. Therefore, if you use the low power objective, the specimen on the slide will appear 10 x 10 or 100 times its actual size.

The lens in the high power objective usually magnifies forty times. Therefore, if you use the high power objective, the specimen on the slide will appear 10 x 40, or 400 times its actual size.

Work with your microscope until you can coordinate the movements of its various parts. A good specimen for practice is a tiny scrap of newsprint.

LOOKING AT NEWSPRINT UNDER A MICROSCOPE

Materials: A scrap of newsprint with the letter "e" on it.

Follow this procedure: Place the newsprint in the middle of a glass slide. Lay a cover slip over it. Place the slide on the stage of your microscope so that the newsprint is over the opening. Switch to low power and look at it.

You will observe: The "e" will look upside down and backward and much

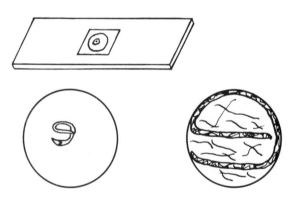

larger than it appears to your unaided eye. Under high power you won't even see the "e" as a letter! It has been magnified so many times that it shows up as heavy black lines crossed with fibres of the paper.

As you already know, the "e" is magnified 100 times under low power of the microscope, 400 times under high power. It appears to be upside down and backwards because straight light rays from the "e" on the slide pass through the double convex lens in the objective and are bent. (Light waves passing from a thinner medium, such as air, to a denser medium, in this case a solid glass lens, are always bent.)

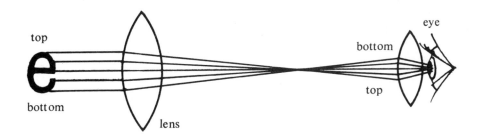

These bent light rays converge (come to a point) in the microscope tube. They then continue into the slightly curved lens in the ocular and up into your eye (see diagram).

OBSERVING A SINGLE HUMAN HAIR

Materials: All you will need besides your microscope, a glass slide and a cover slip is a lone strand of hair.

Follow this procedure: Pull a hair out of your scalp. Place it in the middle of the glass slide and cover it with a cover slip. Put the prepared slide on the stage of your microscope.

Use low power first, and then high power.

You will observe: A long shaft composed of two layers. The point at which the hair was attached to the scalp is cuplike and is called a *root*.

The hairs on your head have their roots in the lower layer of the scalp. The root is actually a collection of cells in the scalp from which the hair grows.

The color of your hair is due to pigment, coloring matter in the cells of your scalp. Hair becomes grey when pigment fails to form at all.

THE STRUCTURE OF COTTON FIBRES

Materials: A small piece of absorbent cotton (just enough to fit between your thumb and forefinger), a glass slide, a cover slip, a medicine dropper, a glass of ordinary tap water.

Follow this procedure: Tease a few strands of absorbent cotton apart and place them on a drop of water in the middle of a glass slide. Protect this with a cover slip. Put the prepared slide in the middle of the microscope stage. Observe it first under low power, and then under high power.

You will observe: The cotton fibres appear transformed into large strings or tubes under low power. Of course, they are even larger under high power.

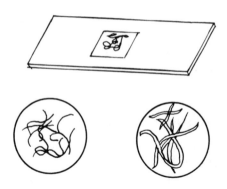

Absorbent cotton is composed of many individual threads that are matted together. But under the microscope each fibre shows up as a separate thread, so that you can see the true composition of the cotton.

THE INTRICATE STRUCTURE OF FISH SCALES

Materials: Get some small fish scales from your grocer or fish dealer. To keep them from drying out, wrap them in moist kitchen paper towelling. You will also need a medicine dropper and a glass of water.

Follow this procedure: Put two drops of water in the middle of a clean glass slide. Put a fish scale in the water and hold in place with a cover glass. Observe first under low power, and then under high power.

You will observe: The dried fish scale that looks so tiny and unglamorous in your hand shows up under the microscope as a beautiful sculptured structure. Concentric ridges will appear, making this single scale resemble a complicated abstract drawing by a modern artist.

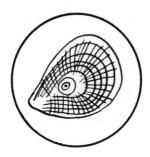

Scales grow on a fish's body in the same manner as the overlapping shingles are placed on the roof of a house. The attachment of the scale is toward the head of the fish. The wider, overlapping part of the scale faces the tail of the fish. This overlapping arrangement of scales provides the fish with a coat of armor, as protection, and also with a hard, sleek covering for cutting through the water as it swims.

Each *species* (closely related group) of fish produces scales that have a characteristic pattern. If you wanted to observe hundreds of fish scales and catalogue them, you could eventually tell the species of a fish just by examining a single scale under your microscope. The pattern of lines on the scale would reveal the fish's family to an experienced eye.

TYPICAL CELL STRUCTURE — "EMPTY" CORK CELLS

Materials: A thin piece of the rounded side of a bottle cork, a sharp, single-edged razor or a paring knife (with Mother or Dad's permission), a glass of tap water and a medicine dropper.

Follow this procedure: Slice off a very thin piece of the cork. Put this in two drops of water on the slide and cover with the cover slip. Try to slide one edge of the cover slip slowly on the slide, so it can settle; this will help prevent bubbles forming on your slide. Place the prepared slide on the microscope stage.

Use your low power objective and get the specimen in focus just at the edge of the cork slice where it is likely to be the thinnest.

You will observe: Tiny empty "boxes" with stiff walls.

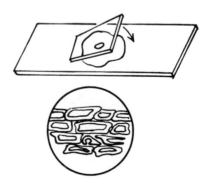

These "boxes" are *cells*. Everything living is composed of either one cell or of many cells, containing living matter called *protoplasm*. This is a thick, jelly-like fluid, and it is the physical basis of all life. But since the living matter of the cork has died, its cells are empty. They no longer contain the miraculous and still somewhat mysterious protoplasm.

In addition to protoplasm all cells have a *nucleus*, a dense round structure usually in the middle. This is the "heart" and "brains" of the cell, for it directs all of the cell's activities. A cell cannot live, nor can it divide or reproduce itself, without a nucleus.

LIVING PLANT CELLS FROM AN ONION SKIN

Materials: Ask your mother for a small paring knife and permission to use it. Get a small piece of fresh onion, a medicine dropper and mix a solution of iodine and water, called "dilute iodine."

Follow this procedure: With the medicine dropper place a drop of dilute iodine in the middle of the glass slide. With the paring knife, carefully peel off a tissue-thin layer from the top piece of onion. Place this in the drop of iodine on the slide. Carefully put the cover slip over it.

Place the prepared slide on the stage of your microscope. Observe first with low power, and then with high power.

You will observe: Many rectangular boxes. These are the building blocks of all living plants and animals—the cells.

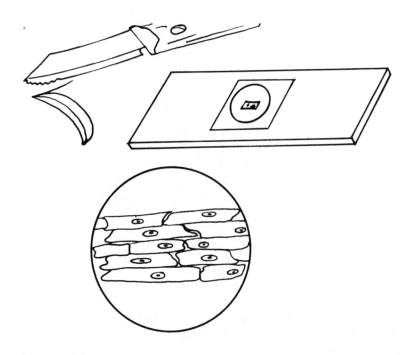

All the functions that are necessary to keep a plant alive are performed individually in each cell and coordinately by all the cells working together. As you know, every cell is made up of living matter that we call protoplasm. The dark spot that you see in the middle of each cell is known as the nucleus. Without this nucleus the cell cannot function. The nucleus helps the cell to grow and is especially important in producing new cells of the same kind so that the same kind of plant can grow.

EXAMINING GREEN PLANT CELLS – ELODEA

Materials: Besides a medicine dropper or pipette (a narrow glass tube operated by suction), and a glass of tap water, you will need an aquarium plant called "elodea." This is a leafy aquatic plant which you can buy at any pet supply store.

Follow this procedure: Put two drops of water in the middle of a clean glass slide. Tear off one green leaf from the stem of a healthy elodea plant and carefully place it in the water on the slide. (Make sure that the leaf is not folded.) Cover with a cover slip. To keep bubbles from forming in the water, place the cover slip gently at one end, as you did in preparing empty cork cells as a specimen.

Put the slide under the microscope and observe under low power first, and then under high power.

You will observe: Large brick-shaped cells containing small, oval green bodies.

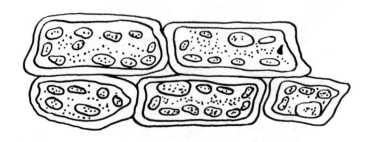

Elodea, like all other living plants, is made up of living cells. In addition to protoplasm and a nucleus, the cells of green plants contain green bodies called *chloroplasts*. In turn, chloroplasts contain a green substance called *chlorophyll*. Green plants, both water-living and land-living, are able to manufacture their own food because they contain this valuable life-supporting chemical, chlorophyll.

Green plants are the original source of all our food. They provide food directly for us and indirectly, too, because they provide food for the animals we eat. It is the chlorophyll in green plants that makes possible a wonderful process called photosynthesis, which you will learn more about on page 37. Bear in mind that all life depends on this green chemical—chlorophyll.

OBSERVING CELLS OF THE HUMAN BODY — CHEEK-LINING CELLS

Materials: A flat-ended toothpick, a pipette or medicine dropper and a dilute iodine solution.

Follow this procedure: Using the medicine dropper or pipette, place a drop of iodine solution in the middle of a clean glass slide.

Gently scrape the inside lining of your cheek with the flat end of a clean toothpick. Put the scrapings in the drop of iodine solution on the slide.

Observe first under low power, and then under high power of your microscope.

You will observe: Small cells, some folded and some flat, scattered either by themselves or in groups in the microscope field. The nucleus, or organizing mechanism, of each cell will appear as a small brown spot in the middle.

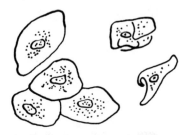

The inside lining of your cheek is made up of a thin tissue composed of living cells. (Your entire body is made up of different kinds of tissues of living cells.) When you scraped them with the toothpick, the upper cells separated from the rest of the tissue.

New cells will grow to replace those that are scraped off whenever you eat or drink something.

Part II: THE WORLD OF PLANTS

By now you have examined the simplest structural units of living things, cells; you know something about the mysterious life-giving substance called protoplasm; you have seen chloroplasts containing chlorophyll, the equally mysterious substance in the leaves of green plants on which all life is dependent for food. You are well under way in your study of biology.

Now you will venture into the vast and varied world of plants. Of course, some plants are well known to you—the apples or oranges you eat, the seaweed washed up on the beach, the sweet peas which may grow in your mother's garden or those energetic dandelions that make a nuisance of themselves by popping up all over the lawn in spring and summer.

But there are hundreds and hundreds of *other* plants, less well known than these. Some grow low on the floor of woods and forests, or on the sides of rocks and trees. Among these are the ferns, mosses and mushrooms which you will study soon. Some plants (elodea, for example) grow only in water; others, like the familiar oak, elm and maple trees, grow only on land. It won't surprise you to hear that plants vary in size, but do you know *how much* they vary? The giant redwood trees in California sometimes grow as high as 300 feet. On the other hand, there are many plants so small that you cannot see them without a microscope. Among these are various kinds of bacteria and plants called "algae" which live in ponds and streams.

Many discoveries await you in the following pages. You will learn how green plants manufacture their own food and how they manage to reproduce and replant themselves—by flying to their new homes on "wings," by sticking to the coats of animals and in countless other unique ways. You will find out why the different parts of plants (roots, stems and leaves) grow as they do and what part each plays in the life of a plant. You will even be introduced to a strange, insect-eating plant called a *Venus flytrap*.

In these pages, too, you will find out how you can grow plants under unusual conditions. Surprising as it seems, a common bath sponge will support pant life, as will an ordinary drinking glass or a plastic bag.

Equipment you will need

To carry out your investigation of the world of plants you will need very little that cannot be found around your house. Besides your microscope, an inexpensive magnifying glass or hand lens will be valuable, as will several test tubes and a holder in which to keep them. A terrarium, a fish tank filled with earth and used for raising plants, will be useful for some of the studies described in this section.

As the world of plants opens up under your careful and curious investigation, you will be more and more intrigued at the variety of forms plants take and at the variety of ways in which they take care of themselves.

GROWING ONE-CELLED MICROSCOPIC ORGANISMS — BACTERIA OF DECAY

Materials: A piece of raw potato (peeled), a few seeds of either beans or peas, two test tubes and a test tube holder, tap water.

Follow this procedure: Soak the small piece of potato in a test tube of water. Do the same with the bean or pea seeds. Leave the test tubes open and exposed to air for three days. Then put a plug of absorbent cotton loosely in each test tube. Keep the tubes in a comparatively warm place for the next few days.

Place a drop of the water from each test tube in the middle of a clean glass slide. Carefully cover with a cover slip and observe, first under the low power of your microscope, then under high power.

You will observe: Hundreds of large, harmful bacteria. They will be especially clear under high power.

Bacteria that cause the decay of dead plant and animal matter live as *spores* (masses of protoplasm with or without cell walls) in the air and even on plants. When they get warmth and moisture, they become active and feed on dead plant or animal cells, actually breaking them down. This process results in decay.

Some bacteria of decay are useful because they make soil rich for planting purposes by breaking down the cells of plants and animals that have died. The materials of which these cells had been composed return to the soil to be used as nourishment by new growing plants. This is nature's means of fertilizing soil. The action of bacteria in breaking down the cells of dead matter prevents the waste of important minerals that all living plants need in order to grow successfully. In turn, plants provide animals, including human beings, with food containing important minerals. All animals need minerals for the growth of different parts of the body.

OBSERVING BACTERIA OF DECAY

Materials: Dried lima beans, water, a jar with a tight-fitting cover and a medicine dropper.

Soak some beans in a glass of water for several days. Then cover the jar and keep it in a comparatively warm place for the next few days. Use your medicine dropper and take off some of the fluid at the surface. Put a drop or two on a clean slide. Cover carefully with a cover slip. Focus and observe, first under low power of your microscope and then under high.

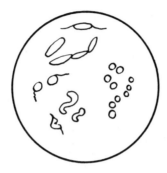

You will observe: Many large bacteria.

Bacteria that are inactive are always present in a spore form in the air and on objects both living and nonliving. The spore form is similar to the state of hibernation that the bear and frog sink into to carry them over a cold winter.

Bacteria of decay develop protective spore coats around themselves until the conditions for growing are good. To grow, bacteria need food, moisture, darkness and warmth. They find these conditions in living plants and animals that have died and have been buried in the ground, or in water.

The bacteria of decay then break through their hard, protective spore coats and start to feed and grow. The dead plant and animal tissues upon which they feed are broken down into their original elements and compounds. This process is known as decay. Usually an offensive odor accompanies decay. This is due to gases that are given off during the breaking down process.

STUDYING SIMPLE FRESH-WATER PLANTS — ALGAE

Materials: A wide-mouthed glass jar, dilute iodine solution, and a medicine dropper.

Follow this procedure: Collect water from a pond in a wide-mouthed glass jar. Keep this at room temperature. Expose the jar of pond water to the sunlight for several hours each day for a week.

Then place a drop of pond water culture in the middle of a clean glass slide. Add to it a drop of dilute iodine. Place a cover slip carefully over the drops on the slide.

Observe first under low power, and then under high power of your microscope.

You will observe: Several types of very simple green plants called algae. Many will be stained blue-black within their cells. Some will have only one cell and others will seem to live in groups or colonies or strands.

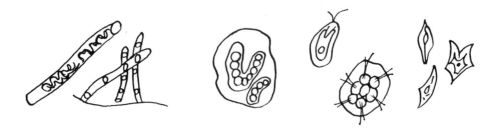

Algae are the simplest water plants which contain chlorophyll, that chemical which is necessary in the production of food for all forms of life. Some algae live only in fresh water and others only in salt water. These plants (like all green plants) can manufacture food in the form of a simple sugar. But plants cannot store sugar in their cells. Within a cell, the sugar is miraculously changed by a chemical process into starch. Starch can be stored for future use. Dilute iodine stains the starch to a blue-black color.

Scientists have been seeking a way to strain large quantities of these important green plants out of the water. It's possible that algae may someday be an important source of food for human beings.

GROWING YEAST PLANTS

Materials: A cake of yeast or a package of dried yeast powder, five teaspoons of molasses, a half-pint jelly jar with a cover, tap water, a medicine dropper, a toothpick.

Follow this procedure: Fill the jar two-thirds full of tap water. Dissolve five teaspoons of molasses in the water. If you use cake yeast, crumble one-fourth of the cake in the molasses and water solution. If you use yeast powder, pour about one-fourth of the contents of the package into the solution. Put the lid on the jar. Set it in a warm place for about 48 hours.

Then, with the medicine dropper, put a drop of the yeast-molasses mixture in the middle of a clean slide. Using the toothpick, spread the drop of water on the slide so that it covers a space in the middle about the size of a small coin. Carefully cover this with a cover slip and observe under the microscope.

You will observe: Yeast cells with small "buds" growing from them. Some will grow as you watch them. Chains of buds will appear right before your eyes.

Yeast is a plant whose body consists of only one cell. When there is sufficient food (the molasses in this case), each yeast plant will grow to its full size. Then new little yeast cells will grow from the fully grown cell. The new small cell is called a "bud." Sometimes it remains attached to the parent cell, and itself produces buds. On the other hand, it may break off from the parent cell, but it will still produce buds of its own.

With only one parent yeast plant, you have grown new yeast plants. The means of reproduction you have observed is called "budding."

PRODUCING SPORES FROM BREAD MOULD

Materials: Half a slice of white bread, a pint jar with a cover, tap water, dust from a window sill, a pair of tweezers.

Follow this procedure: Thoroughly wet the piece of bread. Put it in the jar. Sprinkle some dust on the surface of the moist bread. Screw the lid on the jar and set it in a warm place for several days.

When "mould" appears, use the tweezers to transfer some of the grey fuzz and black spots from the bread to a drop of water in the middle of a glass

slide. Cover with a cover slip. Observe first under low power, and then under high power of your microscope.

You will observe: Under high power the black spots will appear as round cases filled with smaller black spots. The grey fuzz is a branching stemlike growth that holds the black cases to the bread.

The balloon-like sacs containing the small black specks are *spore cases.* The tiny black spots are the actual spores of mould. They are very light and are carried about by air currents. They often settle in dust.

When a bread mould spore lands on a piece of moist bread, it will send out tubelike stems (the grey fuzz) and will grow into a new mould plant.

The air is always filled with spores of bread mould. But they need food and moisture for successful growth; a piece of moist bread provides just the conditions under which these spores thrive.

A strange and fascinating discovery was made by Sir Alexander Fleming, a Scottish scientist, before World War II. He found that a certain kind of bread mould produces a liquid which has the power to destroy some disease-causing bacteria. He called this liquid *penicillin.* The mould that produces penicillin and other "wonder drugs" is now grown in laboratories and used in medicines to treat (and often to cure) such diseases as tuberculosis and pneumonia.

EXAMINING EDIBLE MUSHROOMS

Materials: Fresh mushrooms, a sharp paring knife (with permission to use it), kitchen paper towelling.

Follow this procedure: First observe the whole mushroom. Then cut off the cap and turn it so that you can see the underside.

You will observe: The entire mushroom is a shade ranging from tan to brown. There are thin tissues that look like the separated pages of a book on the undersurface of the cap.

The cap rests on a thick, fleshy, stem-like part that grows securely in rich, moist, leaf-covered soil in shaded forest land.

The mushroom is called a *fungus.* It contains no green coloring matter, or chlorophyll; therefore it cannot manufacture its own food. It gets its food from the dead plant matter in which it grows. It also gets its moisture from the rich soil in which it grows.

The page-like structures on the underside of the mushroom cap contain small spores. When the mushroom is fully grown, these spores burst out of

their cases and are distributed by the wind. If the soil on which they land is rich and moist, each spore will take root and develop into a new mushroom plant.

There are many different kinds of "mushrooms." Some are the edible kind which you are now observing. Mushrooms are fascinating plants, and they grow in a variety of intriguing ways. There are some that grow like shelves on the cooler, shaded side of trees in moist wooded areas. These are called "shelf" or "bracket" mushrooms. Others are called "puffballs" because their caps look like closed ball-like structures.

There are over 60 varieties of edible mushrooms. But there are also some which are poisonous to man as well as to insects and other animals. The most common poisonous mushroom is known as the Amanita. It can easily be distinguished from its edible relative for it has a cup-like structure at the bottom of the fleshy stem and a ring of tissue hanging just below its smoky brown or smooth grey cap. One type of Amanita has a wart-like, yellowish-orange cap.

BUILDING A GLASS-ENCLOSED GARDEN OR TERRARIUM

Materials: An empty fish tank, coarse gravel or small pebbles, sand, rich humus or leaf mould (sometimes bought under the name of "garden loam"), a glass sheet to cover the terrarium, tap water, various ferns, mosses and fungus plants you will collect yourself outdoors.

Follow this procedure: Place a layer of gravel or small pebbles about one inch deep on the bottom of the tank. Over this spread about half an inch of sand. Then, over the sand, spread a third layer of humus or garden loam about one inch deep.

Collect low-growing plants from the rich, moist soil in a thick forest or, if you can't get to a real forest, from any local area that is thickly wooded. These will probably be mosses, ferns and other simple plants. When you pick a fern or moss plant, include some of its native soil around its roots. If you wrap each plant lightly and carefully in wax paper, it will not dry up before you are ready to plant it in your terrarium.

Firmly transplant or sod each little plant in the top loam layer. Water your terrarium generously so that the water level is about halfway up the gravel layer. Now, cover the tank with the sheet of glass.

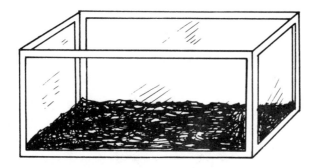

Place your terrarium in partial light, never in direct sunlight. The glass cover helps to keep moisture in the tank but if you see evidence of dryness, add more water from time to time.

During the winter months, it is advisable to keep the tank under an incandescent or fluorescent light bulb for several hours each day.

You will observe: Your low-growing forest plants will thrive as long as they have a rich soil, sufficient moisture and mild sunlight.

Best of all, when you lift the lid of your terrarium, you will smell the delicious fresh fragrance of a forest after rain.

GROWING MOSSES IN YOUR TERRARIUM

Follow this procedure: Collect moss plants from cracks in shaded walls, or moist ground under trees and from any cool, heavily wooded area. Look for low green plants that resemble a carpet of green. Wrap the moss plants with a small amount of soil from around their roots in wax paper or newspaper. You can transplant these mosses in your terrarium.

You will observe: A moss plant can be identified by its tiny green stem with a cluster of green leaves encircling it. At the tips of the leafy stems and hidden by the leaves are the plant's reproductive organs. Little tan spore cases on slender stalks grow from among the green leafy stalks.

The spore cases each contain tiny spores. Each spore, when it falls on rich, moist soil, will become a new moss plant.

Mosses are valuable to man primarily because they hold down soil in a forest and absorb water the way that a sponge does. Therefore, they prevent the soil from being washed away by hard rains. Peat moss, partly carbonized vegetable tissue formed by the partial decomposition of moss, is valuable as a fuel when it is pressed and dried. It can then be used in place of coal. In Ireland especially there are famous bogs from which peat moss is cut and used as fuel.

GROWING FERNS INDOORS

Follow this procedure: Collect ferns from a moist wooded area. Uproot them as you did mosses, keeping intact some of the soil around their roots. Be careful, and dig deeply; the fern's stem sometimes grows as deep as six inches under the surface of the soil. Wrap each fern with its attached soil in moist newspaper, wax paper or a plastic bag.

Transplant the ferns with their attached soil in your terrarium or in clay flower pots. If you use pots, prepare them first by covering the bottoms with one inch of coarse gravel and then adding an inch of garden loam, humus or leaf mould. Plant each fern on top of this and fill the rest of the pot with a mixture consisting of equal parts of sand and garden loam.

Keep the plants and soil moist, but not wet. Ferns should be kept in partial light, not in direct sunlight. Common ferns will grow well under these conditions.

You will observe: Small dots, sometimes the shade of rust, will appear on the backs of the fern leaves, which are also called "fronds." The presence of these dots indicates that a leaf is fertile, and if you examine them under a microscope, you will see separate spores.

Ferns are among the oldest types of plants to appear on our earth. They do not produce true flowers. The dots on the backs of some fern leaves are *sori* (plural of *sorus*) and they contain spores. Each spore will grow into a new fern plant if it falls on moist, rich soil.

About 300 million years ago giant fern plants (fern trees) lived on the earth when it was hot and swampy. They formed large forests that covered most of the earth. Giant tree ferns grew about 30 or 40 feet high.

During an ancient era called the Carboniferous Age, great layers of these fern trees died and their remains accumulated in the swampy lands in which they grew. Still later, movements of the earth and the additional pressure of layers of rock sediments (soil) on top of the ferns formed beds of coal. Scientists have estimated that it took about 300 feet of compressed giant tree ferns to form 20 feet of the coal which we find in mines today.

MAKING A COLLECTION OF DRIED FERNS

You may want to make a collection of delicate fern plants to mount in an album or scrapbook. If so, collect the ferns just as you did the ones you transplanted to pots or to your terrarium. Remember, ferns grow in moist, wooded, shady areas.

Follow this procedure: To press or dry your collection of ferns, place each one between sheets of newspaper and lay it between heavy books. After it has dried, slip each fern inside a plastic envelope or between pieces of the sticky cellophane wrapping paper your mother probably uses in the kitchen. Using sticky cellophane tape, you can then mount each envelope on a separate page in a scrapbook or on sheets of unlined paper in a notebook. You may want to print some basic information about each fern underneath the appropriate envelope. A collection of dried ferns is fun to make, and you'll be surprised at how much you'll learn in the process of gathering and mounting your ferns.

There are many varieties of ferns, but the most common are the Christmas fern, the cinnamon fern, the sensitive fern and the maidenhair. There are also

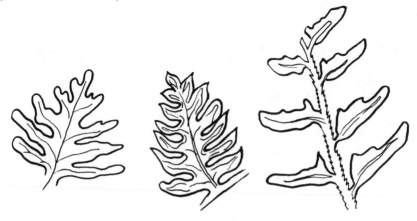

two attractive relatives of ferns. One is the horsetail rush, often found growing along railroad tracks. The second is the club moss. This plant is often used as a Christmas decoration because it resembles a miniature low-growing pine tree.

If you discover the horsetail rush and the club moss and decide to include

them in your fern display, take only one plant of each. Both these plants are passing out of existence, or becoming "extinct" in some areas. As a beginning biologist, you will want to be careful to preserve them.

THE PARTS OF A TYPICAL FLOWERING PLANT

Materials: Almost any common house or garden plant will be a fine specimen for this study. Perhaps there is a flowering geranium growing in a pot on your window sill, or a clump of African violets. A miniature rose bush is also a good subject, as are green pea or green bean plants. When you have found a plant to study, look at it closely, without removing it from wherever it is growing.

You will observe: The roots of the plant pushing down to grow beneath the soil. Growing above the soil are the stems, the green leaves and the flowers.

All true flowering plants consist of roots, stems, leaves and flowers.

The roots keep the plant anchored in the soil and provide it with nourishment, for they absorb water containing important minerals to be supplied to the parts of the plant growing above the ground.

The stems support all the parts of the plant above soil. The water absorbed by the roots passes upward through tubes in the stem so that it can be used to feed other parts of the plant.

A plant's green leaves "breathe" for the plant and they also manufacture its food. You will learn more about this on pages 39–40.

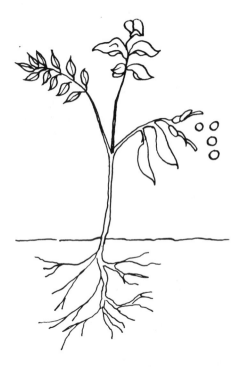

Flowers are the most attractive and, in a way, the most intriguing part of any plant because they produce "fruits" which, in turn, contain the seeds from which new plants of the same kind grow. Flowers contain the reproductive organs of the plant; both the fruit, which provides protection and nourishment for the seeds, and, of course, the seeds themselves, originate in the female part of the flower.

Each seed contains a baby plant (known as an "embryo") as well as food for the embryo. If conditions are suitable, the embryo will grow into a new young plant.

STUDYING A TYPICAL ROOT—A CARROT

Materials: Three fresh carrots, a sharp knife, red ink or vegetable dye (which you can get from your mother or at a nearby store), a glass of tap water, medicine dropper.

Follow this procedure: Cut one carrot across in the middle. (You have made a *cross section.*) Cut the second carrot in half vertically. (This time you have made a *longitudinal section.*) Now, cut off the tip of the third carrot and place the cut end in a solution of water containing a dropper full of red ink or vegetable dye. Let it soak for 24 hours; then make a longitudinal section of the soaked carrot.

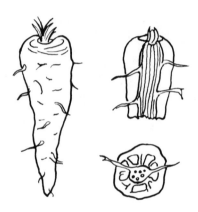

You will observe: In the cross section small rootlets (or secondary roots) will radiate from the central core of the carrot toward the outside. In the longitudinal section, you will see the central core and the secondary roots extending the entire length of the carrot up toward the beginning of the stem.

When you examine the carrot which you stained, you will see the red color in the tubes of the carrot's central cylinder extending from the tip end to the fatter top of the carrot root.

A carrot is actually a *taproot* (a major root which grows downward vertically and gives off smaller roots growing from its sides). It not only stores some food for the plant (and for you, too), but it also absorbs soil water containing valuable minerals. This water travels up into the stems of the carrot plant, and from there to the leaves. The leaves need water and minerals so that they can manufacture food for the entire plant.

Radishes, turnips, parsnips and beets are also familiar taproots.

THE BINDING FORCE OF ROOTS

Materials: An envelope of radish or mustard seeds from your local variety store, florist or nursery, two paper cups, about two cups of rich soil.

Follow this procedure: Soak six seeds in water for several days until they begin to sprout. (They are now called "seedlings.") Fill each paper cup with

soil to about three-quarters of its capacity. Plant the seedlings and let them grow for two weeks. Careful! Water them sparingly.

You will observe: The extensive root systems of the seedlings. Try to pull up a shoot. All, or most of the soil in the cups will come loose with the roots, and the soil mass will have taken the shape of the paper cup.

The roots of plants hold down soil so that it cannot easily be blown away by wind or washed away by rain or running water. The binding force of roots prevents *erosion*, the loss by wearing away of precious top soil.

OBSERVING THE CIRCULATION OF WATER FROM ROOTS TO LEAVES

Materials: A stalk of celery with its leaves attached, a glass of tap water, several drops of red ink or vegetable dye.

Follow this procedure: Dissolve eight drops of red vegetable dye or red ink in a half glass of water. Place a stalk of celery with its leaves attached in this solution, and let it stand overnight.

In the morning, observe the leaves. Pull out a "string" from the celery stem, and make a cross section of the stalk.

You will observe: The leaves have red markings; the "strings" of the celery stem are red, and there are red dots, too, along the outer edge of the cross section of the celery stem.

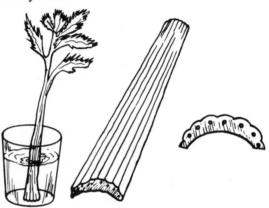

Here is your proof that the mineral-bearing water absorbed by a plant's roots travels up the stem and into the leaves. The tubes through which the water passes are called *ducts.* As you know, the leaves of a plant need water and dissolved minerals as "raw materials" in the manufacture of food for the plant.

STUDYING THE VEIN STRUCTURE OF VARIOUS LEAVES

Materials: A stalk of white celery with its leaves attached, a blade of grass (or a grass leaf), leaves from common trees such as oak, birch, chestnut or maple; red ink or vegetable dye, a glass of tap water and a hand lens, sometimes called a magnifying glass. (You can buy a hand lens at an art supply store, at a large bookshop or stationery store.)

Follow this procedure: Place the celery stalk in a glass of water in which you have dissolved about eight drops of red ink or dye. Let it stand overnight, so that you can examine the leaves the next day.

For studying the other leaves, use your hand lens. Notice how the veins branch out from the leaf stem to all parts of the leaf.

You will observe: In the celery leaf red color will appear in definite branch-like structures. The veins in the leaves of celery, as well as of oak, birch and chestnut, move from the leaf stem into a single main vein called a midvein. From here, branching veins spread to all other parts of the leaf.

However, the structure of veins in a grass leaf differs from that of a celery leaf. Notice how the veins of a blade of grass are patterned in a parallel formation from the leaf stem throughout the leaf.

When you look at the maple leaf, you will see still another intriguing pattern. Here, the main veins seem to radiate from the leaf stem, much as your fingers do from the palm of your hand. From these main veins branches lead to all parts of the maple leaf.

The type of vein pattern that a leaf has is called "venation," and it is characteristic of the kind of tree on which the leaf grows. For example, all oak leaves have a similar shape and the same kind of venation. This is also true of birch leaves, maple leaves, chestnut leaves and so on. The venation of oak leaves is different from that of maple leaves.

Leaf veins contain a set of tubes that conduct soil water (with its accompanying minerals) from the roots and stems of the plant to all the cells in the leaf. You know already that this water is used to manufacture food for the entire plant. The veins also contain a set of tubes that conduct the food prepared in the leaf cells to all other parts of the plant for nourishment.

MAKING A COLLECTION OF TREE-LEAVES

Materials: An old newspaper, several small plastic envelopes or a roll of sticky cellophane wrapping paper (the kind your mother uses in the kitchen), cellophane tape, a scrapbook and fresh green leaves from as many different trees as possible.

Follow this procedure: Dry or press the leaves as you did the plants in your fern collection. Place each leaf between two pieces of newspaper and press it for about a week under the weight of large books. When pressed, put it in an individual plastic envelope or cover it with a sheet of sticky cellophane wrapping paper.

Sort the leaves into groups. You can classify each according to the type of venation (above), the general shape of the leaf's outline or according to whether it is *simple* or *compound*. A simple leaf has only one blade on a leaf stem. On a compound leaf, there are many blades on a single stem. If you have difficulty sorting your leaves into categories, you may want to consult a handbook on botany.

After you have sorted them, use sticky cellophane tape to attach each leaf in its proper place in a scrapbook or notebook. It's a good idea to use a loose-leaf notebook, because you can add new specimens to each group whenever you like.

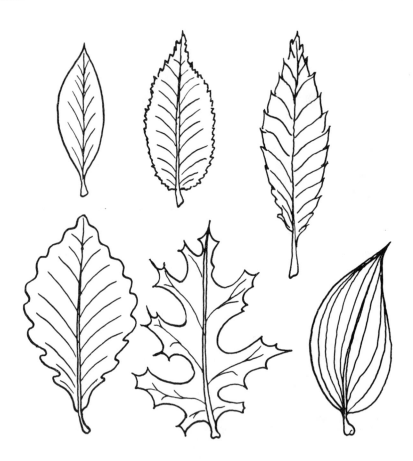

The variety of leaves on different types of trees is tremendous. Some trees bear simple leaves, with only one blade to a leaf stem. Among these are oak, birch, maple, elm and sycamore. On the other hand, the locust, the ash and the horse chestnut have compound leaves, on which a single leaf stem carries many leaf blades.

The general shape of a leaf is also a good means of classifying it. The

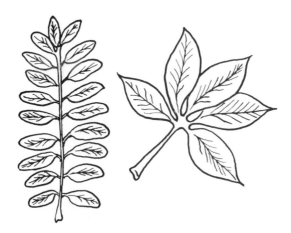

edges of some leaves are smooth, other are scalloped. Still others are jagged, or cut up like teeth.

The kind of leaf a tree bears, its type of venation and the character of a leaf's edge all help to identify the type of tree on which the leaf grew.

HOW A GREEN LEAF PRODUCES FOOD – PHOTOSYNTHESIS

Materials: A leaf from a silver geranium or a coleus plant, a double boiler, a solution of dilute iodine (iodine mixed with water), a small amount of alcohol, a saucer, a forceps or an old kitchen spoon. For this experiment, you will have to use the kitchen stove, but be sure to get your mother's permission first.

If you are lucky enough to own an alcohol burner, you can use it for this study—along with a ring stand and an asbestos pad.

Follow this procedure: Fill the bottom of the double boiler with hot water and bring it to a boil. Place a geranium or a coleus leaf in the top of the double boiler and cover it well with alcohol. Remember, though, since alcohol burns quickly, you must never put a container of alcohol directly over a flame!

Set the top of the double boiler over the boiling water in the bottom pan. After a few minutes—as soon as the leaf loses its coloration—turn off the flame. Then, using your forceps or spoon, remove the leaf and put it on a plate. (If the leaf is still green, return it to the top of the double boiler and heat a few minutes more.)

Wash the boiled leaf carefully under slow-running tap water. Lay it flat on the plate and pour dilute iodine over it. After a few minutes pour off the iodine and wash the leaf again in tap water. Clean the plate.

You will observe: The leaf has become either greyish or completely without pigment. But after it was treated with dilute iodine, it turned blue-black. The alcohol in which the leaf was boiled has turned green.

By boiling the leaf in alcohol, you removed its chlorophyll, or food-making substance. And later, when you treated it with dilute iodine, you tested it for the presence of starch. If iodine causes a blue-black shade to appear, you know that the substance you tested contains starch.

You remember that a green leaf is a food-making factory for the entire plant, and that chlorophyll, which makes the leaf green, is the basic machinery of this factory. It puts together raw materials to make a finished product, in this case starch. In the plant, the raw materials are water (which the plant gets from the soil through its roots) and the gas carbon dioxide. A leaf actually breathes through microscopic openings called *stomates* located on its under-surface; this is how a leaf takes in carbon dioxide from the air.

Every factory needs power, or energy, to run its machinery. Sunlight is the source of power for every leaf factory. Without sunlight, leaves would not be able to manufacture food for plants, nor, indirectly, for animals and humans. The first food product that a leaf manufactures is a form of sugar, but the plant changes this sugar to a type of starch for easier storage.

This miraculous food-making process—on which all life depends—is called *photosynthesis.* "Photo" refers to light (in this case, sunlight) and "synthesis" refers to the "manufacture of." The process of photosynthesis is the manufacture of simple sugars by the green plant in the presence of sunlight.

ISOLATING CHLOROPHYLL AND TESTING FOR STARCH IN A LEAF

Materials: A leaf from a green and white coleus plant or from a "wandering Jew" plant (also called Tradescantia), alcohol, a double boiler, dilute iodine, a dish, a forceps or a large kitchen spoon.

Follow this procedure: Remove a green and white leaf from the plant you have chosen. Using the method you just learned in studying how a green leaf produces food, boil the chlorophyll out of the leaf. (Again, be careful not to expose the alcohol to direct flame!) Now, place the boiled leaf in a dish and test it for starch with dilute iodine. Be sure you wash off the excess iodine solution.

You will observe: The part of the leaf that originally was green became blue-black. The part of the leaf that originally was white remained without pigment.

Only leaves or parts of leaves that contain chlorophyll are active in photosynthesis. Therefore, the white part of the leaf you tested did not contain starch, proof that it was not part of the plant's food-making factory.

THE UNDERSURFACE OF A LEAF — STOMATES

Materials: A geranium leaf, a single-edged razor blade or sharp paring knife, tap water, a medicine dropper.

Follow this procedure: With the razor blade or sharp paring knife, peel off as thin a piece of the underneath surface of a geranium leaf as you can. Place it in a drop of water in the middle of a slide. Carefully cover with a cover slip. Observe first under low power of your microscope, and then under high power.

You will observe: Small openings appearing at intervals. Each opening is encircled by two kidney-shaped cells.

These tiny openings are the stomates, through which a leaf takes in carbon dioxide from the air. There are about half a million stomates on an average sized leaf. Each is controlled by two "guard" cells that regulate the size of the opening, depending upon how much carbon dioxide the leaf needs. The guard cells close the opening to prevent the escape of water when the soil is dry due to lack of rain.

The stomates are on the undersurface rather than on the upper surface, so they will not become clogged by dust or insects. Also, if they were on the upper surface, the sun's direct light and heat would tend to cause great loss of water by evaporation, and the leaf would wilt and die.

But some leaves *do* have stomates on their upper surfaces. For example, leaves that grow upright have stomates on both upper and lower surfaces. Water lily leaves (called "pads") float on the surface of the water; they have their stomates on the upper surface. Otherwise the leaves would "drown" because their air spaces would become filled with water.

SHOWING THAT OXYGEN IS A BY-PRODUCT OF PHOTOSYNTHESIS

Materials: Two small elodea plants, two wide-mouthed jars, two test tubes, two glass funnels, several toothpicks or wooden splints. If you don't have elodea in your fish tank, you can buy some at a pet supply store.

Follow this procedure: Place one plant in each jar. Invert a glass funnel over each plant. Now fill each test tube with water. Holding your thumb over the opening of the test tube, invert it. Lower it under the water in the jar; take your thumb away and place the test tube over the inverted funnel. Do the same with the second jar.

Place one jar in the sunlight for a day. Place the other in a dark closet. (The second jar is called the "control." It helps you be sure that the results of your experiment are valid.)

At the end of a day carefully remove the test tube from the jar which was in the sunlight. Keep your thumb over the test tube opening. Now, light a

toothpick so that it flames. Blow out the flame, and immediately, while the toothpick still glows, put it in the test tube. Then do the same thing with the test tube kept over the plant that was kept in the dark.

You will observe: The test tube over the plant kept in the sunlight *appears* to be empty, but when you placed the glowing toothpick in it, the stick burst into flame. This happened because the test tube contained oxygen. The toothpick test on the test tube over the plant kept in a closet shows quite a difference! Since this test tube still contains water, the glowing toothpick will sputter out.

It is because of sunlight that green plants are able to manufacture food. As you know, this process is called photosynthesis. But plants not only produce food—as a by-product they give off the gas oxygen. Oxygen is released through the stomates, usually on the undersurface of each leaf.

Oxygen is needed to make things burn. Therefore, since the toothpick placed in the test tube over the plant kept in sunlight burst into flame, you know that oxygen was present.

The oxygen given off by green plants is a necessary part of the air breathed in by all living things. See how great is the importance of green plants! They not only manufacture food for us as well as for other animals, they also return oxygen to the air we need in order to live.

SHOWING THAT GREEN PLANTS GIVE OFF WATER FROM THEIR LEAVES

Materials: A large, healthy leaf from a geranium plant, two glasses or wide-mouthed jars the size of glasses, a shirt cardboard, water, a small amount of vaseline.

Follow this procedure: Cut a piece four by six inches from the shirt cardboard. Punch a small hole in the middle.

Break off a large, healthy leaf complete with its leaf stem (called a "petiole") from the main stem of the geranium plant. Insert the petiole of the leaf in the hole in the cardboard. Place the cardboard with the petiole downward over one glass, three-quarters full of water. Plug the hole in the cardboard with vaseline to prevent evaporated water from the lower glass from circulating upward. Then cover the leaf with the second glass, so that it rests on the cardboard. See the illustration below. Place this arrangement of glasses in the sunlight.

You will observe: After several hours droplets of water will appear on the inside of the upper glass.

The green leaves of plants give off the water they do not need through the stomates in their undersurface. This process is known as *transpiration*.

HOW GRAVITY AFFECTS PLANT GROWTH

Materials: At least 10 bean, radish, pumpkin or sunflower seeds, two small wide-mouthed jars or beakers (ten-ounce or pint-sized jelly jars will be fine), clean blotting paper, kitchen paper towelling, string, some tap water.

Follow this procedure: Soak eight seeds in water overnight. Now you will construct and plant a "tumbler garden." Line the insides of both jars with a piece of blotting paper cut to fit. Fill the middle of each jar with crumpled towelling. Now, saturate both the blotting paper and the towelling with water. Pour off the excess. Unless the blotting paper is kept moist, your seeds will not grow.

Push four soaked seeds between the glass and blotting paper at the top of each jar.

After the seedlings have grown an inch above the top of the jars, set one "tumbler garden" on its side.

You will observe: The seeds will *germinate.* In less than a week they will grow into baby plants with green leaves.

A few days after you have set one jar on its side, examine it. The little seedlings will have turned on their stems so that they will be growing upward again.

Stems and leaves of plants tend to grow not only in the direction of the light but also *away* from the center of the earth and the *force of gravity.* This pattern of growth has an interesting name. It is called *negative geotropism,* meaning "away from the force of gravity."

WHY LEAVES TURN COLOR IN THE FALL

Materials: All you need are several leaves from the same tree, but collected at different times of the year. A botany handbook or a biology text-book will be helpful for identifying leaves you are not sure about. Then, too, you will need the materials you used previously in making collections of pressed ferns and leaves.

Follow this procedure: In summer collect the green leaves of maple, ash, elm, oak, sycamore, poplar and other trees. Carefully dry and press these leaves between newspaper under heavy books. Collect fallen leaves of the same trees in the early fall. Compare the colors of these leaves with those of the pressed green leaves. Make a third collection of fallen leaves in the late fall, and compare them to the others.

You will observe: The early fall leaves of elm, ash, sycamore and some maple trees will be yellow or brilliant orange. Sugar and red maple leaves will be deep, vivid red. Some oak leaves will be purple, others scarlet.

The late fall leaves of all these trees will be dull, dry, brown and will fall apart or crumble easily.

After a summer of manufacturing food, the chlorophyll bodies (chloroplasts) of green leaves die because they have completed their job. Excess food made during the summer is stored in the trunk and roots of the tree for use during winter.

There are pigments other than green in most leaves, but they are hidden under the chlorophyll. However, when the green color dies, these other pigments show up. This is what accounts for the vivid shades of autumn leaves.

Then, in late fall when the weather becomes cold, the other pigments and the cells of the leaves die. Dry, crumbly brown leaves are actually "dead." The falling of these leaves from the tree in late fall prepares the tree for winter cold and for snow. Otherwise, winter temperatures would freeze the water in the veins of the leaves, and this would eventually harm the tree itself.

Trees whose leaves die and fall off annually are known as *deciduous* trees. But the leaves of other trees, called *evergreens*, do not lose their leaves during fall. The leaves of evergreens are more like needles, with a thick, protective, waterproof, waxy covering, than like what we usually think of as leaves. Some familiar evergreens are pines, firs, hemlocks, spruce and tamarack trees.

STUDYING A FLOWER – THE SWEET PEA

Materials: If there are no sweet peas in your garden, you can buy a spray inexpensively at the florist's shop. Use a hand lens or magnifying glass to examine the flower's lovely structure.

Follow this procedure: After you have carefully observed the flower, gently pull the petals away from the center and expose the organs inside.

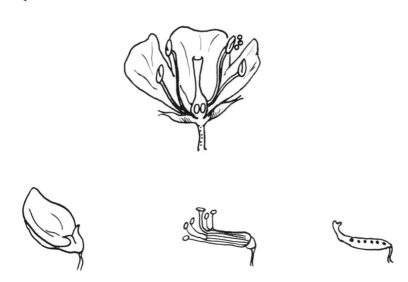

You will observe: Delicate white or pink petals that are mildly fragrant. These petals attract insects to the blossoms.

Tiny, green, leaf-like structures called *sepals* at the base of the petals protected the bud before it blossomed into a flower.

The reproductive organs that you exposed are protectively covered by the petals. You will see a collar-like formation of *stamens;* these are the parts of the flower which give rise to male cells. Each stamen has a structure at its tip called an *anther* which provides the *pollen.*

Remove the collar of stamens, and you will see the *pistil* of the flower. The base of the pistil is called the *ovary.* If you split the ovary apart with your fingernail and examine it with your hand lens, you will notice tiny *ovules* (egg cells) that may become future seeds—in fact, they may become green peas!

Its fragrant petals attract bees and other insects to the sweet pea flower where they suck the flower's sweet nectar (a liquid produced by plants to attract insects). If a bee lands on a flower he accidentally gets pollen on his hairy body. If he then flies to another flower of the same kind, he will transfer some of the pollen to it. This process is called *pollination*.

The pollen grains stick to the top of the pistil. Each pollen grain contains a male cell. The male cell passes down a tube in the pistil until it reaches an ovule (the female egg cell). The male cell combines with the female cell, resulting in a *fertilized* egg. Now the egg is capable of becoming a new sweet pea plant.

Each fertilized egg or ovule now becomes a seed. In the case of the sweet pea, the seed is a green pea. As the seeds grow, the ovary of the flower becomes increasingly larger until, finally, the enlarged ovary in the pea flower becomes a pea pod, containing pea seeds.

All flowers contain the reproductive organs of the plant, usually surrounded by protective petals and sepals. If you examine a gladiolus, an apple blossom or a geranium, you will find the same parts as in the sweet pea, but they will be arranged a little differently.

EXAMINING SEED PODS – "DRY" FRUIT

Materials: Get whole string beans and green pea pods from the vegetable store.

Follow this procedure: Examine the unopened pods of the green pea and the string bean. With your fingernail split the pods open down the bottom division or "seam."

You will observe: The "dry" fruits which contain the seeds of the pea and string bean plants. The pea seeds and bean seeds are attached to the pods by a tiny stem-like part.

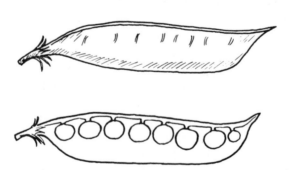

Although you would never include pea pods and string beans in a fruit bowl, each of these is actually the fruit of the plant. Each contains seeds that can be planted to produce a new sweet pea or string bean plant.

They are called "dry" fruits because they do not contain the pulpy, fleshy material found in other fruits—apples, for example. All nuts, including the coconut, and grain seeds such as wheat and rice are also known as "dry" fruits.

By a miraculous act of nature, the ripe pods spring open and "shoot" the green peas (seeds) and string bean seeds out and away from the parent plant. If the seeds fall to the ground, each may grow into a new plant.

EXAMINING THE SEEDS OF "FLESHY" FRUITS

Materials: All you need is a fresh apple and a sharp paring knife.

Follow this procedure: Cut the apple down the center the long way.

You will observe: The juicy, pulpy mass surrounding a group of hard black seeds.

 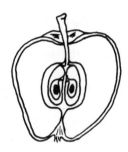

An apple is a "fleshy" fruit because it is juicy and pulpy. Each fleshy fruit contains either a seed (as does a peach, for example) or several seeds that have hard coverings. Each apple seed can be planted to produce a new apple tree.

Sometimes fruit seeds are planted accidentally, just as the bee accidentally pollinates flowers. Some animals eat the fleshy part of a fruit and leave or discard the hard covered part. You, too, eat the fleshy part and throw away the tiny or hard center seed. If it falls to the ground, it may grow into a new plant. Grapes, peaches, pears, oranges and melons are familiar fleshy fruits.

THE STRUCTURE OF SEEDS

Materials: Fresh green peas, dried lima beans, a hand lens, a jar or glass, tap water.

Follow this procedure: Soak lima beans in water for 24 hours.

Remove the green peas from their pods and examine the outside of the peas.

Then, with your fingernail, remove the tough outside covering of both kinds of seeds and separate the two halves.

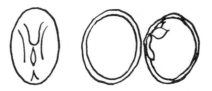

You will observe: Each whole seed is covered by a tough skin-like coat. There is a scar where each was attached to the pod. Just above that scar is a tiny hole in the seed coat.

When you separate the two halves of the seeds you will find, neatly tucked in one half, a small structure with two distinct parts.

The skin-like covering of the whole seed is its "coat." It serves the protective purpose of any coat.

The two halves of the seed are called *cotyledons*. They contain stored food for the baby plant.

Nestled between the two seed halves (cotyledons) is a tiny structure called the embryo. If the seed is provided with enough moisture and warmth, the embryo will grow into a baby plant.

The lower, hook-like part of the embryo will grow to become the roots and part of the stem of the plant. The tiny leaf-like part of the embryo will become the part of the stem above the ground and the first two green leaves of the new plant. The growing embryo will live on the food that is stored in the cotyledons until it has grown its first green leaves above the ground. The green leaves will then manufacture food for the young plant by the process of photosynthesis.

HOW SEEDS PLANT THEMSELVES

Materials: In the late fall of the year collect the following seeds: maple, ash, thistle, elm, dandelion, milkweed, burdock or cocklebur, "beggar's tick," snapdragon. Also get an acorn, a coconut and a cherry pit. You may want to use a botany handbook to help you identify these different seeds.

You will observe: The maple seed has double wings. The ash and elm seeds have single wings. The dandelion seed has a feathery structure resembling a parachute. Both the thistle and the milkweed seeds have soft, wispy plumes and tufts. Burdock or cocklebur and "beggar's tick" have hook-like barbs. The acorn is nut-like. Snapdragon seeds, like green pea seeds, are encased in pods from which they are later "shot." Cherry seeds are buried in a fleshy fruit mass. The coconut seed is enclosed in a lightweight porous shell called a "husk."

Nature has shaped seeds and given them special structures so that they can be carried away from the parent plant to places where each can develop into a new plant.

If seeds were to fall too close to the parent plant, they would be crowded out by the parent and would not get enough nourishment or space in which to grow.

Seeds with double or single wings are carried by the wind and "sail" on air currents until they fall or are blown to the ground.

The dainty light, feathery parachute of the dandelion and the tufts of milkweed and thistle are moved or wafted by slightly moving air. Eventually, of course, they land on the ground.

The hooks on "beggar's tick" and burdock catch onto the fur or hides of animals. They find earth in which to grow when they are brushed off or fall.

As you know, the seeds of fleshy fruits are distributed after animals or humans eat the fruit, discarding the seeds.

The coconut palm drops its ripe seeds on the beach. When the tide comes in, they are picked up by ocean waves and deposited somewhere else on the beach.

RAISING SEEDLINGS IN A TUMBLER GARDEN

Materials: Three dried lima beans, three dried corn grains, two glasses or wide-mouthed jars, blotting paper, paper towelling, tap water.

Follow this procedure: Soak the lima beans and corn grains for two hours in a glass of water.

Prepare a "tumbler" or "pocket" garden just as you did in your study of how gravity affects plant growth. (See page 42.) Plant the lima beans in one jar and the corn grains in the second one. Keep them moist. Place the gardens in a warm, dark place (perhaps a closet) until green leaves appear. You can watch the various stages of growth through the glass.

You will observe: The seed coats of each seed will split open. Roots will develop and grow downward. The stems of bean seeds will arch upward, pulling with them the cotyledons. The first green leaves will pop out from between the two cotyledons. Then, the stem will straighten up, and the first pair of green leaves will appear.

The first leaves of the corn seed will seem to be wrapped around the stem. They will grow straight upward. Unlike bean seeds, these have only one cotyledon which remains attached to the roots.

The embryos in seeds will grow into new plants only if they are provided with moisture and moderate warmth. We call this growth stage, from the embryo to the young plant seedling with its first green leaves, *germination.*

GROWING SEEDLINGS IN A SPONGE GARDEN

Materials: A natural bath sponge, a few radish or mustard seeds, tap water, string, a clothes hanger, a drinking glass, an indoor clothesline or a suitable stand from which to suspend the sponge.

Follow this procedure: Soak seeds overnight at room temperature in a glass of water. Soak the sponge in water, too, and allow the excess to drain off. Tie a string around the sponge and suspend it from something, perhaps an indoor clothesline. Now, place seeds in the holes of the sponge.

This is your garden. Keep it suspended at room temperature in moderate light (away from the direct light of a window).

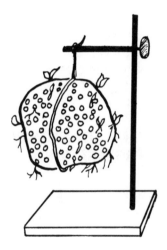

You will observe: In a few days each seed will begin to germinate. Roots will be seen growing downward, and leaf stems growing upward from various parts of the sponge.

A seed contains an embryo and stored food for the first stages of growth of the baby plant. If the embryo has the right conditions, moderate warmth and moisture, it will begin to grow. The roots will grow downward toward the center of gravity (a "pulling" force in the center of the earth). The stems and the new leaves will grow upward, away from the center of gravity and toward the light.

The baby plant uses the food stored in the seed until it has developed its first pair of green leaves. With these, it no longer has to rely on seed-stored food. Now it can manufacture its own.

OBSERVING SEEDS SOWN IN DIFFERENT TYPES OF SOIL

Materials: At least 12 mustard or radish seeds, four small flower pots, different kinds of soil containing gravel, sand, clay, and humus.

Follow this procedure: Soak a dozen seeds in tap water overnight.

Fill each of the flower pots with a different type of soil. Plant three seeds in each prepared pot. Water each one until it is moist but not soaked. Every other day you should water the seeds.

You will observe: In less than a week, seedlings will begin to grow in each pot. If you have kept them in the light and given them sufficient water, they will continue to grow, but the seedlings in the pot containing humus will grow the fastest and will be the healthiest.

Before the seedling grows above the ground, the baby plant gets all the nourishment that it needs from the seed. But after the first green leaves appear, they need minerals as well as water and carbon dioxide to help them produce food for the plant. Of the four types of soil you used, only humus contains the minerals that the growing plant needs.

GROWING PLANTS FROM PARTS OTHER THAN SEEDS – VEGETATIVE PROPAGATION

Materials: A white potato, a sweet potato, a carrot, an onion, a narcissus bulb, a garlic head, a four-inch branch of English ivy, philodendron or geranium. You will also need sand, toothpicks, a dark green jar, two saucers, two additional glass jars.

Follow this procedure: Cut the white potato into three parts; each part should contain several "eyes." Plant each piece in wet sand.

Suspend a sweet potato by placing it in the neck of a jar of water. If you put several toothpicks in it, they will support the potato as they rest on the rim of the jar. The water should cover the bottom of the potato.

Cut about one inch off the top of a carrot. Set this in a small saucer of water. As the water evaporates, add more—never let the dish get dry.

Place an onion and a head of garlic each in a separate jar or glass of water. Use toothpicks to keep them partially submerged, just as you did with the sweet potato.

Place a narcissus bulb so that it rests partially in wet sand or pebbles.

Cut off a small branch (about four inches) of ivy, philodendron, or geranium just below a node, the point where the leaves join the stem. Place this in a dark green jar of water.

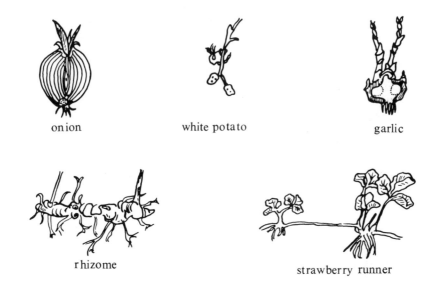

onion   white potato   garlic

rhizome   strawberry runner

You will observe: Stems, leaves and roots will grow from the "eyes" of the white potato pieces. Stems and leaves will grow from the top of the sweet potato and rootlets from the bottom. Lovely green stems and feathery leaves will sprout from the top of the carrot slice. Long green leaves will grow out of the top of the onion, white roots from the bottom. From the top of each garlic clove, long green leaves will grow and from the bottom of each, white roots. The same type of growth will occur in the narcissus as in the onion.

After about a week, roots will begin to grow from the cut end of the ivy (philodendron or geranium) that is under water.

You can often grow an entirely new plant from a part of a plant other than its seed. Professional gardeners prefer this method because it is faster than raising plants from seeds, which are slow to germinate. In addition, you can be more sure what will grow from a part of a known plant than from commercially packaged seeds. A new plant growing from a part of a plant other than the seed will be almost identical to the parent. Plants grown from seeds may have unforeseen combinations of traits or even very undesirable features.

A white potato is actually a thick underground stem. The eyes in the potato are stem and leaf buds. Each piece of potato containing an eye has enough stored food to nourish the buds until green leaves grow from them. Then the green leaves manufacture food for the new plant by the process of photosynthesis.

You probably remember that a carrot is a taproot. Like the potato, it contains a great deal of stored food. The stems and leaves grow from the top, feeding on the stored food as they develop.

You started a narcissus from a bulb, but did you know that an onion and a garlic clove are bulbs, too? Each is actually a mass of fleshy leaves surrounding a short, small stem. Each may grow small bulblets, and a new plant may result from each bulblet.

After roots appear at the cut end of the stem of ivy, philodendron or geranium, you can plant the "cutting" in humus. An entire new plant will develop. From one ivy, geranium, or philodendron stem, you can have many. This is called propagating a plant with a *cutting*.

STARTING SEEDLINGS IN A PLASTIC BAG

Materials: Seeds, a drinking glass, tap water, a small flower pot, a plastic bag (without ventilation holes), several paper clips.

Follow this procedure: Soak the seeds in a glass of water for a day. Plant or "sow" them in humus in the flower pot. Soak the soil thoroughly after you have put in the seeds.

Put the pot in a plastic bag and fold over the open end several times. Secure the folded opening with paper clips. Place the enclosed pot in a warm, dark part of your room.

You will observe: In a week or ten days the first green leaves will appear.

Now place the pot, still enclosed in its bag, in the sun. Do not remove the plastic bag for any reason, not even to water the plant.

After the seedling is about three inches high, remove the plastic bag and water regularly. Keep the flower pot in the sunlight.

The plastic bag prevents moisture from escaping. There is enough air in the bag to support the life of the germinating seeds. As it germinates the plant uses and re-uses the moisture originally provided it.

After the seedlings are established, about three inches high, the plant is ready to manufacture its own food. Now it needs more carbon dioxide and more water than when it was germinating.

The supply of carbon dioxide and of moisture within the plastic bag is no longer enough to support the plant's activities. The bag must be removed and the plant exposed to air and sunlight.

ADVENTURES WITH MEAT- AND INSECT-EATING PLANTS

Materials: Ask your florist for two bulbs of the Venus flytrap plant and enough peat or sphagnum moss in which to raise them.

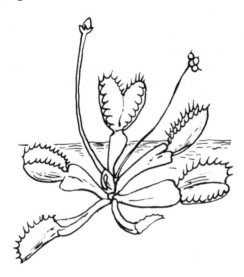

Follow this procedure: Plant the bulbs in a small fish bowl, an aquarium or a large brandy snifter containing peat moss or sphagnum moss. Keep it in sunlight but away from extreme temperatures. Keep the moss moist (but not soggy) all of the time. Use rain water or tap water that has been allowed to stand for a day or two. In warm weather, keep the plant near an open window or outdoors. In cool weather, keep it indoors on a sunny window sill.

When the leaves are fully grown, "feed" them either a small insect that you have captured or a tiny piece of raw, chopped, lean meat.

You will observe: The leaves will snap shut when an insect or a piece of meat lands on them. After the plant is finished "eating," they will open slowly.

Charles Darwin called this strange, rare plant "the most wonderful plant in the world." The Venus flytrap grows with its light green leaves arranged in rosette fashion. Each leaf has two sections which operate on a hinge. There are thorn-like spines at the edges of these leaves.

The Venus flytrap is an insect-eating plant. We call it an *insectivorous* plant. It grows wild in bogs. The special trap leaves have tiny sensitive hairs lining the inside. They also give forth ("secrete") a sticky odorous substance that attracts insects.

An insect unfortunate enough to be lured to the plant lands on the leaf and begins to eat the sticky substance. The tiny sensitive hairs act like triggers, causing the leaves to spring closed, trapping the insect.

Poor insect—it cannot escape. Gradually the soft parts of its body are digested by juices prepared and secreted by the leaf. The plant uses the digested insect body or meat to build protoplasm for cells and tissues.

If you feed the plant chopped meat, it will react the same way as with the insect, and devour a hamburger dinner.

The pitcher plant and the sundew plant are two other fascinating insect-eating plants. These plants grow naturally in the tropics, where there is extreme heat and an abundance of moisture.

Part III: THE WORLD OF ANIMALS

You will not be surprised to hear that animal life is just as varied and just as endlessly fascinating to observe as is the world of plants. You may even think animal life much *more* interesting than plants. The body organs and the life processes of animals are closer than those of plants to the ways in which we ourselves are built and function. And if you are like most people, you will want to know as much as possible about your own body.

Unlike plants, animals do not manufacture their own food. In one way they are less self-sufficient than plants, but in another, they are more so, for animals can move from one place to another under their own power. And there is tremendous variety in the ways they get around. Some hop, some fly, others swim and many others walk or run. Some animals use combinations of these methods. A frog, for example, is equally at home in the water as he is on land. And although a chicken cannot fly for long distances, he travels both by foot and by air.

Described in the following pages are many activities designed to reveal the wonders of the animal kingdom. You will see "invisible" animals, whose bodies consist of a single cell. These animals, protozoa, have to depend on a single cell to carry out all their life functions. This cell does everything, but of course in a much more simple way, that is done by the infinitely more complicated tissues and organs of frogs, birds and human beings. In protozoa a single cell eats, digests food, gets rid of wastes, breathes and reproduces.

Most animals are much more complex than the protozoa. Moths, butter-flies and frogs mature in an unusual way; they pass through several distinct stages of development before becoming what we consider full-grown. The spider is fascinating, too, for the many uses of his fragile web, as is the oyster, which has the gift of producing a gleaming pearl from a grain of sand.

You will study a typical insect, the grasshopper. You will observe the skeletal structure of a fish, you will learn how it is possible for a fluffy yellow chick to develop from an egg. You will collect and arrange your own display of sea animals and sea shells and you will investigate the mysterious little firefly, who makes summer evenings so cheery by flashing his bluish light on and off.

As for equipment, you may want to purchase an aquarium, if you do not already have one, or perhaps a more specialized type of aquarium, a vivarium, especially designed for raising turtles and similar animals. But you already have most of the equipment you will need for the adventures described in the pages that follow.

MAKING A HAY INFUSION TO STUDY PROTOZOA

Materials: Dried timothy grass (a common wheat-like grass called "hay" by farmers), a few dried leaves, a jar of pond water containing scum from the surface of a pond, a small amount of silt or mud-like soil from the bottom of a pond, some uncooked rice.

Follow this procedure: Fill a jar one-quarter full of pond water which includes both scum and silt. Add a few spears of timothy grass and several leaves. Keep the jar uncovered in a warm part of your house for a few days. At the end of that time, add five or six grains of uncooked rice to the water. The combination of timothy grass, leaves and pond water is called an *infusion*.

You will observe: The dried grass and the leaves will begin to decay, perhaps making the water appear a little cloudy. More scum will appear on the surface as time passes. Decayed parts of the hay and leaves will drop to the bottom of the jar. You will probably notice the unpleasant odor of decay that is characteristic of stagnant pools of water.

The plant matter in your jar contains spores of bacteria of decay (see page 20) as well as some one-celled animals enclosed in cases called *cysts*. Cysts are similar to the spores you examined in your study of bacteria. Given moisture and warmth, the one-celled animals come out of their cysts, just as the bacteria come out of their spore coats.

The bacteria feed on the vegetation in the jar and cause it to decay. Similarly, the one-celled animals feed on the decayed matter. As a result, they grow and multiply rapidly. Some of them feed on the decaying rice grains. As long as there is food, the microscopic animals in the jar will thrive, but they will die as soon as the decay on which they feed is used up.

The simple, one-celled animals living in your hay infusion are known as *protozoa*.

OBSERVING PROTOZOA

Materials: Your hay infusion, a medicine dropper, a small piece of absorbent cotton. This is a microscope study, so you will need a clean slide and a cover slip, too.

Follow this procedure: Place a few strands of absorbent cotton in the middle of a clean slide. The cotton strands will tend to keep the more active protozoa confined so that you can observe them. Very carefully, so as not to stir up the infusion, take some water from the bottom of the jar with your medicine dropper.

Place a drop of this water on the cotton lying on your slide. Cover carefully with a round cover slip. Observe first under low power, and then under high power of your microscope.

Now, prepare a second slide just as you did the first. There is one difference, though; this time take your specimen from the *surface* of the infusion. Compare what you see on the two slides.

You will observe: After your eye becomes accustomed to the lightness of the water, you will see tiny forms of moving animal life. Some protozoa will be darting back and forth across your field of vision. Some will seem to be tumbling over and over, like the rolling barrels in a "fun house." Others will glide lazily along, while still others will seem to ooze sluggishly. You will see protozoa of many different shapes and sizes.

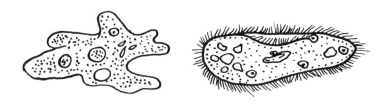

These tiny bits of independent life (protozoa) are animals whose bodies consist of only one cell. Varieties of these one-celled animals may be found in pools, ponds, lakes, rivers, even in oceans and seas. Although many live by themselves independently, some love company and exist in groups. There are types of protozoa who feel at home at the bottom of a body of water and other types who prefer the better lighted part of the water near the surface. However, all protozoa serve as food for larger, water-living animals.

The two best-known types of protozoa are the amoeba and the paramecium. The former resembles an irregularly shaped blob of protoplasm. It changes its shape constantly as it oozes slowly from one area to another. The paramecium, on the other hand, never changes shape. It looks very much like the sole of a shoe, and it darts swiftly around the water.

A particularly interesting type of protozoa has a tiny, chalk-like cell around its one-celled body. The famous chalk cliffs of Dover, on the southern coast of England, are made up of countless numbers of chalk-like cells that were washed up by the sea after the soft-bodied animals themselves died.

Some protozoa are disease-producing animals. We call them *parasites*. Malaria is one of several diseases caused by a parasitic protozoa.

MAKING A COLLECTION OF SEA SHELLS AND ANIMALS

Materials: The next time you go to the seashore make a collection of interestingly shaped and tinted sea shells and of some of the small sea animals you may find washed up on the sand. When you are home again and want to preserve your collection of these objects, you will need sticky cellophane paper, a large roll of absorbent cotton and a cardboard box big enough to hold your shells and sea animals.

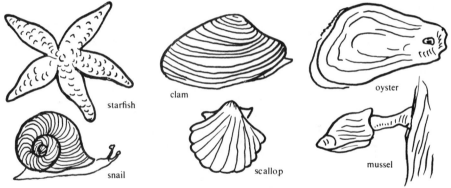

starfish
clam
oyster
snail
scallop
mussel

Follow this procedure: Starfish should be weighted down in a flat position and allowed to dry in the sun. Sand dollars will not have to be weighted, for they are flat, but they, too, should be dried in the sun as should crabs and young crayfish. If you prefer, you can preserve crabs in a tightly covered jar containing alcohol. The shells of oysters, clams, mussels and snails should be boiled in water in an enamel pot for a short time, and then completely dried.

Label each specimen (you can attach a piece of paper to it with sticky cellophane tape), cover it with transparent kitchen wrapping paper and place it in a large cardboard box about half-filled with absorbent cotton.

Starfish, sand dollars, crabs, oysters, clams, mussels, snails and crayfish inhabit the relatively shallow areas of bodies of salt water. Since their bodies are soft and they do not have internal skeletons or backbones, they are called *invertebrate* animals.

Naturally these animals need some means of protection, particularly since their bodies are soft. To provide this, their body cells secrete the hard protective substances we call shells. Crabs and crayfish shed their outgrown shells as their bodies grow larger and produce new and larger shells to fit as needed. On the other hand, clams, oysters, mussels and snails do not leave their shells as they grow. Their bodies secrete new cells to add to the original ones and more shell material to add to their size. When a crab has just formed a new shell that has not yet hardened, it is called a "soft-shelled crab." This term designates a stage in the development of a crab.

All over the world the sea animals you have collected are valued as a source of food.

STUDYING A STARFISH

Follow this procedure: Examine the dried starfish in your collection of shells and sea animals.

You will observe: There is a round opening in the middle of the underside of the starfish. Along the undersurface of each "arm" of the animal there are two rows of little stem-like suction cups.

The central opening in the underside of the starfish acts as a mouth that pulls food directly into the sac-like stomach of the animal.

The suction cups along its arms help the animal stick to the hard surface of larger animals and to rocks as it moves its muscular arms in locomotion.

An oyster provides a delicious meal for a wily starfish. And the starfish's means of catching and devouring his prey is quite fascinating.

The starfish slowly moves up on the unsuspecting oyster who may be just relaxing at the bottom of a shallow part of the sea. The starfish crawls over his future meal and wraps himself firmly around the two-part shell of the oyster. The oyster quickly snaps shut its double shell and holds it firmly closed. The muscles of the oyster are very strong, so the shell stays closed tightly. You might think that closing his shell would protect the hapless victim, but eventually he has to open it so that he can "breathe." By taking in water and taking from it the oxygen he needs, the oyster stays alive.

As soon as the starfish feels the muscles of his future meal relaxing, he relaxes his own grip but still remains wrapped around the oyster. When the space between the two oyster shells is large enough, the starfish quickly inverts (turns inside out) his stomach through his mouth opening and pushes it between the parted shells. The strange "inside-out" stomach of the starfish produces juices that quickly digest and absorb the soft body of the oyster. His meal completed, the starfish withdraws his stomach and crawls away to enjoy an after-dinner rest. All that remains of the oyster is a pair of empty shells.

THE OYSTER AND THE PEARL

Materials: Get a live oyster from a fish market.

Follow this procedure: Examine the oyster.

You will observe: The living, fleshy part of an oyster is soft and boneless. This is also true of the bodies of his close relatives, the clam, the scallop, the mussel and the snail. The outer shells of these animals provide shelter and protection against other sea animals.

Usually the oyster can wash out a grain of sand or the hard shell of a much smaller animal that might be swept into his own shell by the water. But sometimes a grain of sand or a tiny hard shell gets stuck between his shell and the oyster's soft body. This irritates the oyster. The soft tissue around the irritating object secretes a liquid called nacre or "mother-of-pearl." This liquid flows around the grain of sand and hardens to form a smooth protective layer over it.

The oyster continues secreting layer upon layer of mother-of-pearl until a mature pearl is formed. It takes a long time—perhaps as long as five to ten years—for a pearl to be produced. Of course, the size of a pearl depends on how long it remains among the secreting tissues of the oyster.

The hard, glistening, irridescent inner surface of the oyster's shell is mother-of-pearl, too. It provides a thick coating to protect the animal's soft body from what would otherwise be a rough shell surface.

STUDYING A GRASSHOPPER — A TYPICAL INSECT

Materials: A large jar, a square of cheesecloth, a rubber band—and a grasshopper. You can catch one fairly easily in early summer in an empty lot or a field.

Follow this procedure: Place the grasshopper in a large jar with fresh grass and twigs. Cover the jar with a piece of cheesecloth secured by a rubber band. When you see that the grass is dying, add fresh grass with drops of water on it and fresh twigs. Grass growing in a piece of earth is good for this purpose because it will stay fresh longer than cut grass.

Examine the grasshopper with your hand lens.

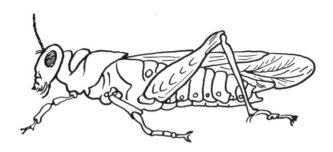

You will observe: The body of the grasshopper has three distinct parts. They are called the head, the thorax (the middle part) and the abdomen (the rear section). All three sections are covered with a hard substance.

You will see a large pair of eyes and a pair of delicate "feelers" that are called *antennae* at the top of the head. The biting mouth parts are easy to find just at the bottom of the insect's head.

Attached to the thorax are three pairs of legs and two pairs of wings. The third, thickest pair of legs is the jumping pair. The top pair of cover wings are long and narrow and rather stiff. The lower wings are delicate, transparent and fan-like when they are open for flight.

If you look closely with your hand lens at the abdomen of the animal, you will see a tiny opening on each of the sections (segments) that make up the rear. These openings exist in pairs, one on each side of a segment. They are called *trachea*, and it is through these openings that the grasshopper breathes.

If the grasshopper is a female, she will have a long, pointed, divided segment at the end of her abdomen for depositing her eggs in the soft ground. If it is a male, the final segment will be bluntly rounded.

The grasshopper is a good example of an insect, for it has all of the characteristics of this type of animal.

When you pick up a bug, you can determine whether it is a true insect if it has the following characteristics:

1. A hard, outer body or shell-like covering which biologists call an *exo-skeleton* (outside skeleton). This protects the soft inner parts of the insect's body.

2. Three separate body parts called the head, the thorax, and the abdomen in that order.

3. A pair of antennae at the top of the head. These operate in the way that radio antennae do. They receive messages of sound and motion and guide the insect's flight.

4. Three pairs of walking legs. In some insects, one pair of legs will be specially developed for jumping.

5. Two pairs of wings.

Not all insects have wings that are well developed enough to enable them to fly. Some ants are not equipped to fly. The "walking stick," which looks like a twig when it is standing still, cannot fly.

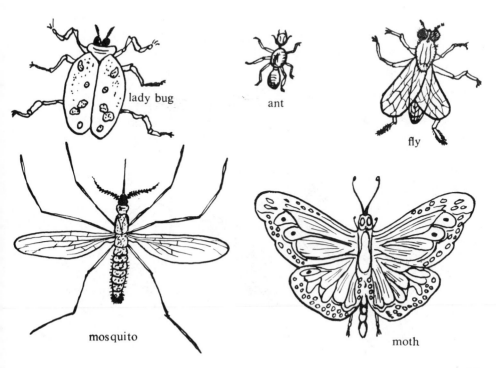

lady bug

ant

fly

mosquito

moth

Some common insects that have all of the above characteristics are the housefly, fruit fly, praying mantis, beetle, lady bug, bee, dragon-fly and the mosquito.

As you know, many insects (bees, butterflies and moths) are useful to man because they help pollinate flowers. Others, like the silk worm moth, produce silk. Of course bees furnish us with honey.

On the other hand, some insects are harmful to man. Grasshoppers and locusts destroy grain and other crops. The tussock, gypsy and leopard moths destroy our shade trees.

Termites cause a great deal of damage by eating through wooden buildings. Carpet beetles and clothes moths are well known pests. Fleas, lice, flies and mosquitoes carry disease-producing germs. Of course, insects such as mosquitoes, wasps, bees and gnats are nuisances because of their stings and bites.

WATCHING A CATERPILLAR BECOME A MOTH OR BUTTERFLY

Materials: A jar containing leaf-bearing twigs and fresh grass, preferably still growing in sod, a square of cheesecloth, a rubber band or short length of string.

Follow this procedure: Catch a caterpillar and place it in the jar filled with fresh twigs and grass. Cover the jar with cheesecloth secured with a string or a rubber band. Keep the jar at room temperature. Replace the twigs while the caterpillar is still active.

You will observe: The caterpillar will eat the grass and the leaves on the twig.

After a while, it will attach itself to the twig and if it is the caterpillar of a moth, it will spin a *cocoon* of white silk threads around itself. If it is the caterpillar of a butterfly, it will cover itself with a hard green or brown case called a *chrysalis*.

After several days the moth caterpillar will pull itself out of a hole at one end of the cocoon. If it is a butterfly, the chrysalis case will split open and a lovely butterfly will emerge.

At first the wings of the moth or butterfly will appear to be folded around its body, but as the body dries, the wings will open and spread apart. As soon as it emerges from its cocoon or chrysalis, put the insect in the sun.

Moth and butterfly "babies" pass through several stages of development before they become what we recognize as a moth or a butterfly. These different stages are called *metamorphosis*.

The female moth and butterfly lay eggs on twigs, on leaves and sometimes in the ground. The eggs are very hard to find. They develop first into the worm-like animals which we call caterpillars.

Caterpillars eat ravenously of their favorite leaves and grass; of course, they become fat. Much of what they eat is stored for use during the metamorphosis into an adult moth or butterfly.

While the moth caterpillar is in its cocoon and the butterfly caterpillar is in its chrysalis, they do not eat. Although they seem inactive during this stage, they are turning into adult insects. In this final stage of development their function is to produce more eggs, and they die as soon as they have completed this task.

Moths are harmful only before they become adult moths, that is, when they are in the caterpillar stage. The worm-like caterpillar of the clothes moth, cabbage moth, tomato moth, cotton boll weevil and corn ear moth are all damaging to objects man needs and values.

Most butterflies and moths are useful because they help pollinate flowers.

HOW THE FIREFLY GLOWS

Materials: A wide-mouthed jar containing grass or leaves, a piece of cheesecloth, a short length of string or an elastic band.

Follow this procedure: On a summer evening collect several fireflies. Catch them carefully by cupping your hands over each insect. Put them in the jar and cover the opening with cheesecloth secured by a string or rubber band. After half an hour or so, feel the outside of the jar.

You will observe: The insects have a bluish light that they can flash on and off. Since the light is on the undersurface at the tip end of the body, we might call it a "taillight."

When you touch it, the jar will not feel hot, as you would naturally expect.

Why the firefly's light does not produce heat—as do other lights—is still one of nature's mysteries.

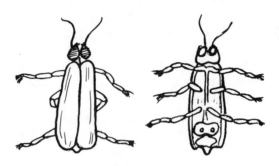

Fireflies, sometimes called "glowworms," are not true flies. They are insects belonging to the beetle family.

The light of a firefly flashes on and off in a definite rhythm, as it seeks its mate in the dark. Recently, scientists have discovered the elements of this insect's strange cold glow. Oxygen, magnesium salts, adenosine triphosphate and two previously unknown substances combine in tiny quantities to form the bluish light of the firefly. Today a few scientists can reproduce this light chemically in their laboratories.

HOW THE SPIDER SPINS A WEB

Follow this procedure: Watch a spider as it spins its web between branches of a tree or from one blade of grass to another. Watch it, too, as it glides over a strand of its web to capture a small fly or a gnat for its evening meal.

You will observe: A definite pattern to the web. Each species of spider spins a particular web pattern slightly different from that of any other species.

You may also see the cocoon in which the female spider has laid her eggs either attached to the web or to the mother's body. In addition, you may see the hard, outer skin of the spider that it shed as its soft body grew in size.

A spider is not an insect; it has four pairs of legs, whereas a typical insect has only three. Spiders, scorpions and mites are called *Arachnids* to distinguish them from their relatives, the insects.

The scientific name Arachnid was derived from Greek mythology. A young Greek peasant girl named Arachne had the audacity to challenge the goddess Athena to a weaving contest. Young Arachne was most skillful, and in a fit of jealous rage, Athena changed the girl into a spider!

The female lays her eggs and wraps them up in a cocoon of silk thread which she herself spins. She uses the same thread as for her web. This is how it is produced: A gland in the spider's abdomen produces a silk fluid. When this fluid is forced out of the spider's body, it hardens into a thin, delicate but strong thread of silk as soon as it comes into contact with the air.

Each kind of spider spins a web that is characteristic of its species. Some webs are extremely elaborate with perfect architectural symmetry and form.

Many fine threads seem to radiate from a central point. Other webs are so simple that they consist of only three or four supporting threads. A lovely sight is a dew-covered web sparkling in the morning sunlight.

An unusual type of web is a "nest" built in the soft earth by the trap-door spider. It is a sac-like nest with a hinged lid that can only be opened by the spider who built it. The nest is so successfully camouflaged that when the trap door is closed, it blends into the surrounding ground. The owner lurks behind the door. When an unsuspecting insect crawls near it, the trap door is quickly opened and then snapped shut behind the insect. Of course, he becomes the spider's meal.

The spider's web serves many purposes. It is the home of the adults and the birthplace of the young. It serves as a snare for the natural enemies which the spider kills and uses for food. A hungry spider will stand quietly at one end of his web, waiting for a fly or mosquito to become trapped in its threads. While the insect struggles to free itself, the spider stings his victim, paralyzing him, before sucking out the insect's life-fluids.

HOW A FISH BREATHES

Materials: A few gills from the head of a freshly caught fish, a dish of water, a medicine dropper, your hand lens.

Follow this procedure: Put the gills in a dish of water. Add a dropper full of water from time to time to keep the gills moist while you are observing them. Observe the feather-like structure of the inner curve of the fish gills with your hand lens. Examine the tooth-like structure of the outer arch of the gills.

You will observe: Gills from freshly caught fish will appear bright red. There is usually a double row of filaments (feather-like threads) on the inner curve. The outer, more solid part of the gills, appears to have a row of fine tooth-like structures.

The feathery filaments of the gills contain tiny blood vessels called *capillaries.* When the fish opens his mouth, water which contains fluid oxygen (and usually some food in the form of tiny plants and animals), is drawn in.

The water passes back over the gills and out through the two flaps (*opercula*) on each side of the fish's head. As the water passes over the gills, oxygen enters the blood capillaries in the filaments. Thus, the gills are the respiratory (breathing) organs of the fish. Unlike human beings and other mammals, most fish have no lungs.

The tooth-like structures on the outer curve of the gills are called *gill-rakers.* They strain out the tiny plants and animals in the water that the fish has swallowed. These tiny forms of life are then directed, as food, into the fish's digestive system.

STUDYING THE SKELETON OF A FISH

Materials: Ask a clerk at a fish market for the backbone of a codfish. Examine it with your hand lens.

You will observe: Separate bones with long projections on each side fitting like a chain, one into the other.

Unlike the sea animals you collected (snails, oysters, clams and the like), the fish is an animal with a backbone. It is called a *vertebrate* to distinguish it from animals that do not have backbones. The backbone is made up of separate small bones (*vertebrae*) which are separated by cushions of *cartilage*, soft bone-like material found, for example, in the human nose. (You may know cartilage as *gristle*.)

The backbone protects the fish's very delicate and important spinal cord. The spinal cord extends from the brain along the back of the fish to its tail and is made up of nerve fibres. The sensitive nerves and cells of the spinal cord are the fish's nervous system, the control center for all its body activities.

The long, sharp bones extending from each side of a vertebra help to hold the fish's muscles in place.

OBSERVING CIRCULATION OF BLOOD IN THE TAIL OF A GOLDFISH

Materials: If you have a fish tank with goldfish, you can carry out this experiment easily. If not, you may want to buy one at a variety store or a pet shop. You can see the circulation of blood in the tail of a goldfish without harming the little fish. Besides a fish, you will need a medicine dropper, a small wad of absorbent cotton, a saucer, a small fish net and your microscope.

Follow this procedure: Soak the cotton in water from the aquarium. Carefully catch a goldfish in the net. While the fish is still in the net, very gently wrap the soaked cotton around the body of the fish, leaving only the tail uncovered. Place the wrapped fish on a saucer and gently cover the exposed tail with a glass slide.

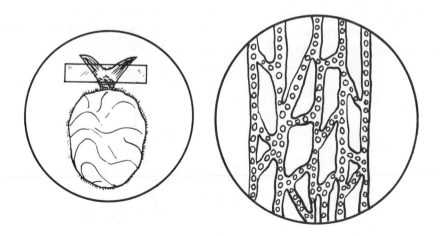

Place the dish on the stage of your microscope so that the tail is under the low power objective. Observe.

Keep the fish tail wet by putting a drop of aquarium water on it every few minutes. Be sure to return the fish to his home in the aquarium immediately after you have observed his tail under the microscope. Be very gentle.

You will observe: The blood flows in tiny tubes from the head region toward the tip of the tail and from the tip of the tail back toward the head.

The fish has a tube-like heart in its "throat" (just behind the gills) that pumps blood to various parts of the body in tubes called blood vessels. The large blood vessels that carry blood *away* from the heart are called *arteries*. The smaller blood vessels that carry blood *back to* the heart are called *veins*. Still smaller blood vessels that branch all over the body are called *capillaries*. Blood brings food and oxygen to all the cells of the body and carries away from these cells many waste products.

THE ELEMENTS OF A "BALANCED" AQUARIUM

Materials: Three large test tubes with rubber stoppers, adhesive tape, two small common snails (Physa), two small water plants (elodea or cabomba), a large-mouthed pint jar.

Follow this procedure: Fill the jar with tap water and let it stand open and undisturbed for about 48 hours. (This is called "aging.")

Fill one test tube two-thirds full of the aged water and place one snail in it. Put the rubber stopper in place and wrap adhesive tape around the top so as to make the tube relatively airtight.

Fill the second test tube two-thirds full of the aged water. Place in it one snail and a sprig of elodea or cabomba. Seal it as you did the first tube.

Fill the third test tube two-thirds full of aged water and place in it only one small sprig of a water plant. Seal it as you did the others.

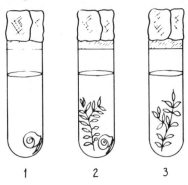

Let these test tubes stand in good light, but not in *direct* light, for several days.

You will observe: The lone snail in the first test tube will die as will the plant in the third test tube. Even though it is sealed, and therefore closed off from the oxygen in the air, the second test tube has provided conditions which sustain life. Both the snail and the plant are alive and perhaps even thriving.

The plant supplies the snail with food and oxygen. In turn, the snail provides the plant with minerals and carbon dioxide. The light provides enough energy for the plant to put together the carbon dioxide, water and certain minerals to manufacture food for itself and for the snail. Now you can see why it is so important to include green plants in your aquarium.

OBSERVING THE METAMORPHOSIS OF A FROG

Materials: Collect frog eggs from the shallow water of a pond early in the spring. Put them in your aquarium or in a large jar of water containing a few pond weeds.

Follow this procedure: Keep the little black and white eggs that are surrounded by a mass of gelatin in the same water until they develop. See that they get sunshine or light from an electric bulb during the daytime hours.

After the fish-like young tadpoles develop from the eggs, feed them bits of boiled lettuce leaf each morning. Be sure to remove the uneaten food at the end of the day so that the tadpoles will not be killed by the decay products of the leftover lettuce.

You will observe: The mass of eggs is surrounded by a transparent gelatin substance that keeps it floating near the surface of the water. The protective gelatin also acts as a magnifying lens, for it concentrates the warm rays of the sun on each developing egg.

After a period of about 8 to 20 days, depending on the amount of sunshine or heat the eggs get, fish-like baby frogs, or tadpoles, will wiggle out of the eggs and gelatin mass. Tadpoles swim like fish.

After about 9 days, each tadpole will develop hind legs. Then, as the tadpoles continue to grow, their tails will become increasingly shorter and front legs will appear. During this time the tadpoles' bodies will begin to look more frog-like.

Finally each tadpole will become an adult frog with two pairs of legs and no tail. Each will try to leave the water in search of a rock on which to sit. Be careful! They may jump right out of your aquarium! Now it's best to take your frogs to the woods and let them free near a pond.

Biologists call the development of frog eggs into frogs a metamorphosis. The process is similar to the transformation of a caterpillar into a moth or butterfly described on pages 66–67.

As the tadpole is developing his legs, his tail gets shorter because it is being absorbed as food. He gets other kinds of food by scraping the leaves and stems of water plants.

In the process of becoming an adult frog, the tadpole lost his gills and developed lungs to take their place. A tadpole breathes only in water, but a frog breathes on land. The frog is called an *amphibian*, a term given to animals which can live on land as well as in water.

It takes about 60 to 90 days for a tadpole to become a full-grown frog. If frog eggs develop into tadpoles in the early spring, it is usually about the first of July that they become frogs. However, the huge, deep-voiced bullfrog usually spends two winters as a tadpole. It takes three years for him to develop fully.

RAISING PET TURTLES

Materials: An aquarium or vivarium (a container of plastic or glass especially designed for raising animals such as turtles), a flat rock or a floating cork, turtle food.

Follow this procedure: Buy two or three small turtles in a pet shop or bring home a small wood turtle from a pond.

If you use an aquarium, it should contain two to four inches of water. Add a cork float or place a flat rock in one corner of the tank as a resting place for the turtles.

Change the water twice weekly to keep it clear and clean.

Feed your turtles small bits of raw fish, ground raw meat or liver. Buy a can of ant eggs and follow the feeding instructions printed on the can. Most turtles will enjoy a small piece of hard-cooked egg, a bit of lettuce leaf, and a small thin slice of raw apple in addition to their regular meat and fish diet.

Both the small green turtles ordinarily available at pet shops and wood turtles will thrive in a well-kept aquarium or vivarium if they are fed properly. But if your turtles become sluggish and inactive toward winter, they may be trying to find a place to hibernate, or rest inactively, until summer. Put their tank in a cool place at this time and do not be disappointed if they remain apathetic and do not eat much. Don't try to force them to eat. When spring comes, your turtles will become lively again and their appetites will return to normal.

When a turtle feels the need to escape or to protect itself, it will pull its legs and head into its hard double shell. This is its natural means of protection.

The shape of the undershell of the turtle is a guide to its sex. If the undershell (properly called the *plastron*) is slightly convex (curved outward) it is probably a female turtle. If the undershell is concave (curved inward), it is a male turtle. If you have a common box turtle, the male can be distinguished from the female by his red eyes. By contrast, the female's eyes are yellow. All male turtles have long claws on their webbed toes, whereas female turtles have short claws.

THE STRUCTURE OF A CHICKEN EGG

Materials: Ask the butcher for several unlaid chicken yolks from the body of a chicken. In addition, you will need a whole chicken egg, a dessert dish, your hand lens.

Follow this procedure: Crack the egg carefully and pour the contents into a dish.

Examine the opened shell and the contents of the egg with your hand lens. Examine the unlaid yolks too.

You will observe: The unlaid chicken eggs resemble clusters of yellow-orange grapes of different sizes.

The shell of the whole egg has the familiar hard outer surface which you have seen in other shells, but there is a thin, tissue-papery membrane clinging to its inner surface. There is a space between the thin membrane and the hard shell at the rounded end of the egg, but at all other places the papery membrane sticks close to the shell.

Now, look at the egg in the dish. You will see the familiar orange yolk in the middle surrounded by the thick, loose "white" of the egg. You will see a white spot just about in the middle of the yolk.

Look hard at two ends of the yolk opposite each other; you will see twisted threads of white, similar to but thicker than the white spot in the middle of the yolk. Around this is the thick white of the egg.

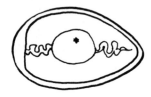

The cluster of unlaid egg yolks was taken from the chicken by the butcher before the eggs were laid. These, of course, are egg yolks.

The white spot in each yolk is the egg nucleus from which a new baby chick might have developed if the egg had been fertilized by a rooster. Eggs are produced in a pair of ovaries in the body of the mother hen.

The yolk surrounding the nucleus provides a supply of food for a developing baby chick. Of course, egg yolks are nourishing food for humans, too.

The white of the egg serves as protection, while the two twisted white cords you saw on the yolk keep it attached to the shell. They act as hammock strings for the developing baby chick.

The papery membrane under the brittle outer shell is also protective. It is thin enough so that air can pass through for the developing baby chick. The outer shell is porous so that air can pass through it to the paper membrane. The outer shell also provides protection for all the internal parts of the egg.

The various parts of the familiar chicken egg are secreted in the body of the hen and poured around the yolk as it is passing through a tube on its way to the outside of the hen's body; the shell does not become hard until the egg reaches the air after leaving the body of the mother hen.

STUDYING THE DIGESTIVE ORGANS OF THE CHICKEN

Materials: Ask the butcher to show you the digestive organs of a chicken. The liver and the gizzard are easy to obtain because they are included among the edible parts of the chickens your mother buys.

You will observe: The tube through which the chicken's food passes before it is digested is similar to the human *gullet.* The liver, which we eat when cooked, is a brownish-red shade and consists of two sections. Unlike the soft liver, the gizzard is very tough and looks like a thick bag. The intestine resembles a sleek coiled tube.

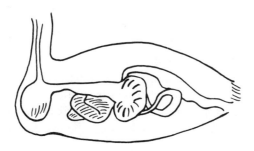

The chicken eats mostly corn and other grains and some small gravel stones. After being taken into the mouth, the chicken's food passes down the gullet into the top of the stomach. It then moves on into the tough organ called the gizzard or crop. There are, in the gizzard, stones or pebbles that grind up the food. Oddly, these stones serve the function of teeth. The chicken's food is chewed *after* it is swallowed, for like other birds, chickens have no true teeth.

Once it has been ground into a fine powder in the gizzard, the chicken's food passes on to the intestine. The liver and other glands supply digestive juices to the small intestine where the food is digested.

If you have a pet parakeet or canary, it is wise to include in its diet tiny pebbles that it can take into its gizzard to aid digestion.

STUDYING THE STRUCTURE OF A CHICKEN LEG

Materials: One leg from an uncooked chicken, a hand lens, a sharp paring knife.

Follow this procedure: Observe the outer skin covering of the entire leg. Use a hand lens to help you identify the various parts. Later, tease off the skin with a paring knife and observe the tissues lying beneath the skin.

You will observe: Most likely, the chicken will not have its feathers but you can see with your hand lens the hole in each bump in the skin from which a feather once grew.

Under the protective outer skin, you will see the "meat" of the chicken leg, arranged in bundles and attached to the bones by bands of tissue resembling elastic. You will see blood vessels among these bundles of "meat." There is a shiny, slippery covering at the ends of the leg bones.

The leg of the chicken is an organ of its body. It is made up of many tissues all working together to do a job. Naturally, the job of the pair of legs is to hold up the rest of the body and to enable the chicken to walk and run.

The skin bears the feathers and also protects the softer, inner tissues.

What we call the "meat" of the leg is really a set of muscles. The thick bands attaching the muscles to the bones are known as *ligaments*. It is the muscles that cause the leg to move.

The blood vessels supply the cells of the muscles with the food and oxygen that they need to give them energy to cause motion.

The ends of the bones are covered with gristle or cartilage so that the joints can move easily. They operate in the same manner as hinges on a door.

Part IV: THE HUMAN ANIMAL

It is exciting to pick up an oyster shell as you walk along the beach and to realize that this shell was once the home of a soft-bodied animal that was capable of making a milky pearl to protect itself against an irritating grain of sand. It is mystifying to watch a fluffy yellow chick crack through the shell of an egg. It is fun, too, to examine the amazingly varied and sometimes comical protozoa through your microscope. All life is fascinating and everlastingly miraculous.

But it is most thrilling of all to learn about your own body and how nature has adapted it to carry on all the necessary life functions, such as digestion and respiration and the circulation of blood. Of course, it isn't possible for us to study the internal organs of the human body. This we leave to students of medicine. But we can achieve a good understanding of our own bodies by studying the animals whose organs most closely resemble ours.

In the experiments that follow, you will study the heart and lungs of a cow and the kidneys of a lamb. In structure these organs are very similar to the corresponding human organs, and they are identical in function. You will learn why you have different types of teeth and how it is that your tongue can distinguish among various taste sensations. Those of you who want to invest in some additional equipment can make a working model of the human chest cavity. What better way to understand the way your lungs work!

Also included among the following experiments are some activities that will show you the differences between human beings and other animals. In the process of seeing how habits are formed and how we learn by a method called "trial-and-error" you will have a lot of fun.

The ability to learn new ways of doing things and to form habits is one of the primary differences between human beings and other animals. You will see for yourself why man's brain makes him superior to all the other animals.

Many of these experiments call for companions. They make lively games for parties or for any slow rainy afternoon—all you need are pencils and paper!

THE HUMAN MOUTH

Materials: A mirror.

Follow this procedure: Open your mouth wide and examine your teeth. Notice especially their different shapes and their positions in the upper and lower jaws.

Feel the inside of your cheeks on both sides with your tongue (just opposite the second upper molar). You will feel a slight bump on each side and a liquid will flow onto your tongue.

Now feel the roof of your mouth with your tongue. Look at it in the mirror. Examine your tongue in the mirror, too. Roll it around. With your tongue, feel the lower surface of your mouth under the tongue. Look at this section in the mirror.

You will observe: You have four essentially different kinds of teeth. The four front teeth in both the upper and lower jaws are square with knife-like or chisel-shaped edges. These are called *incisors*. On each side of the incisors are single, pointed teeth. These are commonly known as "eye" teeth because they are under the eyes, but they are officially called *canines*.

Next to the canines are larger teeth with hill-like projections called *cusps* on their surface. These are your *molars*.

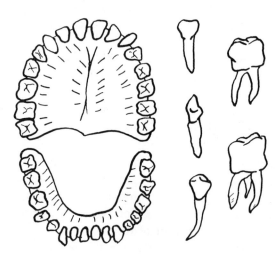

By the time you are 8 or 9 years old, you will probably find 24 teeth in your mouth. Between the ages of 18 and 24 you may develop additional molars called "wisdom teeth."

The slight bumps you felt when you passed your tongue across the insides of your cheeks are the openings into glands called the *salivary glands*. The liquid they secrete is the saliva which flows into your mouth through tubes located at each side of your upper jaw.

The roof of your mouth (called the *upper palate*) is hard when you run your tongue over it and seems to have a slightly ridged bony structure under the moist covering tissue.

Your tongue is muscular and has a rough surface due to the presence of many extremely tiny "bumps."

Each different kind of tooth has a certain shape and size so that it can perform a certain function.

The chisel-shaped incisors are adapted for biting and cutting food.

The canines are especially fitted for holding and tearing certain kinds of food such as meat. Beavers have sharp, ever-growing canines for gnawing wood. Dogs, wolves and similar animals are called "canines," because of their long, sharp teeth for tearing meat.

The large bumpy molars with their hill-like surfaces are adapted for grinding and crushing food.

When you are between 18 and 24 years old, you may develop two additional pairs of molars, one in the upper and one in the lower back of each jaw. These are "wisdom" teeth, and if yours develop, you will have a total of 32 teeth. There is so little room in the human jaw for these large teeth that often they do not grow out of the jaw, but become lodged in the jawbone. They are then said to be *impacted.*

Your tongue is an aid to chewing, because it moves the food around the mouth as it is broken down by the different kinds of teeth. It also helps the food become mixed with the saliva, secreted by glands in both cheeks, so as to make swallowing easier. The rough surface of the tongue is caused by the presence of many tiny "taste buds." Without these you would not be able to distinguish among sweet, sour, bitter and salty tasting foods.

IDENTIFYING FOODS BY TASTE ALONE

Materials: Small peeled cubes of raw apple, carrot, onion, potato, celery and turnip, a pair of tweezers. Ask one of your parents or a friend to work with you on this experiment.

Follow this procedure: If you are the taster, have your assistant blindfold you. Hold your nose (that is, pinch it closed with a thumb and forefinger) while tasting. Your assistant should place each sample food on your tongue, one at a time, and you should identify each one by taste alone. Have your friend make a record of your responses.

Now blindfold the other person taking part in the experiment and go through the same procedure.

You will observe: The taster will recognize several of the foods by taste alone, but not all of them. Some he will not be able to identify.

What we think of as the "taste" of most foods is really a combination of taste and smell. When you hold your nose while tasting, of course you cannot experience the characteristic smell of the food. Perhaps you have noticed that when you have a cold—and your nasal passages are clogged—food seems tasteless. Now you understand why this is so.

DISTINGUISHING TASTE AREAS OF THE TONGUE

Materials: Sugar, salt, an aspirin tablet, four drinking glasses, a small amount of vinegar, tap water, a box of toothpicks or cotton swabs.

Follow this procedure: In each of four glasses prepare one of the following mixtures: a 5% solution of sugar (sweet); salt solution; an aspirin tablet dissolved in half a glass of water (bitter); a 50% vinegar solution (sour).

Before you try this experiment, whether on yourself or a companion (it's more fun to work with a friend than alone), wipe your tongue dry with a clean piece of paper tissue. This will prevent saliva from transferring test substances from the spot where they are applied to other parts of the mouth.

First, dip a toothpick in the sugar solution. Before you taste, roll the toothpick around the rim of the glass to remove excess solution. Touch the toothpick to the tip, middle, the edges and the back of the dry tongue. Note on a piece of paper on which part of the tongue the sensation of sweetness was strongest.

Now, rinse your mouth with cold tap water. Dry your tongue. Using a new toothpick apply the salt solution to the same areas of your tongue. Use the same method for testing the aspirin and vinegar solutions.

Be sure to use a clean toothpick for each solution, to rinse your mouth and to dry your tongue after each taste.

You will observe: Sour tastes are strongest at the outer edges of the tongue, while the taste of salt is felt most sharply at the tip and at the edges. Bitter tastes are sensed most keenly at the back of the tongue, and the sweet taste is most noticeable at the tip.

Sweet, sour, bitter and salty are the only food tastes to which the tongue is sensitive. Certain areas of the tongue react to each, because the taste buds

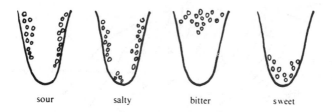

sour   salty   bitter   sweet

in these areas contain nerve endings which respond strongly to a particular taste. All taste sensations other than sweet, sour, bitter and salty are caused by a combination of odor and taste.

OBSERVING A BEEF HEART

Materials: Ask your butcher for the heart of a steer (beef). Besides this, all you need is a sharp knife. Be sure that you have permission to use the knife.

Follow this procedure: Cut the beef heart down the center longitudinally (the long way) so that you can see its four chambers and the blood vessels leading from the broad end, or top, of the heart.

You will observe: The beef heart is a thick muscular organ with cut ends of blood vessels connected to the upper part. Like the hearts of all animals in the group to which man belongs (*mammals*), the beef heart has four separate chambers. The two smaller upper chambers are called *auricles*, and the two lower chambers are called *ventricles*.

The left side of the heart is clearly separated from the right side. The upper chamber of the right side is connected to the lower right chamber by a valve (a sort of "trap door"). The upper left side is connected to the lower left side by a similar valve.

Notice, too, that the lower half of the heart is thicker and more muscular than the upper part and that tubes, the cut ends of blood vessels, all seem to come from the upper part of the heart.

The beef heart is typical of the hearts of all mammals, a class of animals which includes man. The hearts of all mammals are divided into four chambers. The heart acts as a pump, receiving blood which it then pumps out to various parts of the body through blood vessels.

The top right chamber, the right auricle, receives blood from all parts of the body. The blood which flows into the right auricle has been used; that is, it has already functioned in food digestion and in providing fresh oxygen for

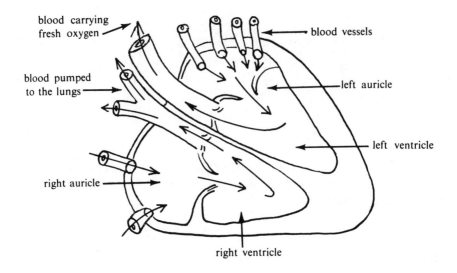

blood carrying fresh oxygen

blood vessels

blood pumped to the lungs

left auricle

left ventricle

right auricle

right ventricle

the cells of the body. As a result, it has picked up waste substances. Eventually these wastes (mostly carbon dioxide) must go to the lungs to be eliminated by exhalation (breathing out) and to the kidneys where the liquid wastes are extracted, to be eliminated in urine. Liquid wastes are also eliminated by the skin, passing off as "sweat."

The blood passes from the right auricle through a valve into the lower right chamber of the heart, the right ventricle. By muscular contractions of the thicker, lower part of the heart, this blood is pumped to the lungs.

In the lungs, the blood exchanges the waste gas, carbon dioxide, for fresh oxygen from the air we inhale (breathe in). This fresh oxygen must be distributed to all the cells of the body.

Blood carrying fresh oxygen returns to the left upper chamber of the heart, the left auricle. From there, it passes through a valve into the left ventricle, the lower left part of the heart.

The thick muscular walls of the left ventricle contract rhythmically, sending the fresh, oxygen-carrying blood to all parts of the body.

In this way each cell of the body of the steer, and of our bodies, too, is supplied by the blood with the oxygen it needs in order to function. Each cell has a means of getting rid of its waste matter, for the blood picks it up and takes it to organs of the body especially adapted to throwing off waste products (the lungs, the kidneys and the skin).

THE HUMAN HEART AND PULSE

Materials: A stop watch or a watch with a second hand, paper and pencil. For this experiment you will need a companion, either a parent or a friend.

Follow this procedure: With the first two fingers (not the thumb) of your right hand, hold the left wrist of your companion. Search for the pulse until you feel it and can count each distinct beat. Record the number of pulse beats per minute while your companion is in each of the following situations:

    lying down, at rest,

    sitting in a chair

    standing

    after jumping up and down in place to the count of 20

    after running up and back down a flight of stairs.

You will observe: The pulse beat is slowest when a person is lying down, and fastest after he has run up and down stairs.

The pulse that you felt when you held your companion's left wrist represents the beats of his heart. Heart beats are the contractions of the thick, left ventricle muscles of the heart as it directs blood to all parts of the body.

When the body is at rest, it requires relatively little nourishment and oxygen; therefore, the heart beats relatively slowly. It beats rapidly (as indicated by an accelerated pulse) when the body requires energy for such activities as running up and down stairs.

MAKING A WORKING MODEL OF THE CHEST CAVITY

Materials: A bell jar (a glass vessel open at the bottom and bell-shaped at the top), a Y-shaped glass tube, a piece of rubber sheeting large enough to cover the open end of the bell jar, two identical rubber balloons, several elastic bands, a wooden button, either a rubber stopper or a cork with a hole through it.

Follow this procedure: Insert the tail of the Y-shaped tube in the cork or stopper. With an elastic band, attach a balloon to each "Y" projection of the glass tube.

Now, insert the stopper or cork, with the Y-shaped tube attached, in the neck of the bell jar. Place rubber sheeting across the broad end of the bell jar and secure with a rubber band.

To make this mechanical breathing apparatus resemble the activity of the human chest, pinch the middle of the rubber sheeting with your thumb and forefinger and gently pull it downward. Then slowly release the sheeting and watch it return to its original position.

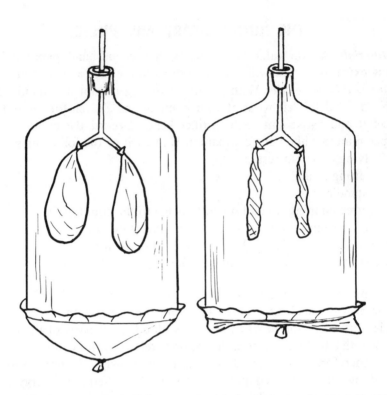

You will observe: The bell jar represents the human chest cavity (the rib cage). The rubber sheeting across the bottom represents the flexible, muscular *diaphragm.* The balloons represent the human lungs.

When the rubber sheeting (the diaphragm) is pulled down, the chest cavity is made larger, and air rushes into the lungs. When we breathe in (inhale) the ribs in a normal chest cavity move outward and the diaphragm moves downward. When the rubber sheeting is released it returns to its original position. This represents the return of the diaphragm (a muscle that separates the chest from the abdominal cavity) to its normal position. In the human body, the ribs move inward, back to place at the same time. This action squeezes the air out of the lungs and we breathe out (exhale).

The waste carbon dioxide in the blood stimulates a breathing center in the brain, the *medulla.* In turn, the medulla stimulates the muscles of the diaphragm to move back upward into their normal position. The ribs, too, move back into place, making the chest cavity decrease in size and putting pressure on the filled lungs. When we breathe out or exhale, our lungs are squeezed together (as illustrated by the collapse of the balloons on your model).

SHOWING THAT CARBON DIOXIDE IS A PRODUCT OF EXHALATION

Materials: Buy a bottle of lime water at a drugstore or soda fountain. You will also need a drinking straw and a tumbler.

Follow this procedure: Take in a deep breath through your nose and mouth. Let the air out by blowing through the straw into the glass of lime water.

You will observe: As the exhaled air bubbles through the straw, the clear lime water becomes milky.

Carbon dioxide, the waste gas given off in exhalation, causes a chemical change in lime water which results in a clouded appearance. Since this is what happened when you breathed through the straw into the lime water, you have proved that carbon dioxide is an element of exhaled air.

SHOWING THAT WATER VAPOR IS PRESENT IN EXHALED AIR

Materials: A mirror.

Follow this procedure: Take a deep breath while standing before a mirror or holding a hand mirror in front of your mouth. Now, exhale against the surface of the mirror.

You will observe: A mist will form on the mirror. Touch this mist, and you will find moisture on the tip of your finger.

In addition to carbon dioxide, water vapor is a waste product of the activities carried on in the cells of your body. As blood flows through the smallest type of blood vessels, the capillaries, it picks up waste vapor. The blood carries this vapor to the lungs to be exhaled, to the skin to be released as an element of perspiration, and to the kidneys to be released in the form of urine.

EXAMINING LUNG TISSUE FROM A BEEF OR CALF

Materials: A paring knife, a wide-mouthed jar, tap water and a calf or beef lung. Your mother's butcher will be able to supply you with the lung.

Follow this procedure: Fill the jar three-quarters full of tap water. Put a piece of animal lung tissue in the water.

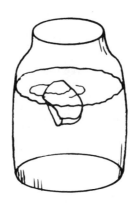

You will observe: The piece of lung tissue will float in the water. Even if you try to force it down, it will bob back up to the surface.

The lung tissue of all mammals is similar. The lungs of mammals contain tiny spaces called *air sacs*. These spaces function like those in a sponge, for they hold the air that is inhaled and collect the air that is going to be exhaled.

USING A THERMOMETER – NATURAL BODY HEAT

Materials: An oral thermometer, alcohol, absorbent cotton.

Follow this procedure: Shake the thermometer down below "normal." Clean it with cotton soaked in alcohol.

Place the thermometer bulb under your tongue. Keep your mouth closed, and leave the thermometer in place for at least a minute.

Remove it and read your temperature as indicated by the strip of mercury running through the tube.

You will observe: If you are in good health, the thermometer will indicate a temperature of 98.6° Fahrenheit. It may be a few tenths of a degree above or below normal without being a signal of illness. A "normal" temperature may vary slightly among individuals.

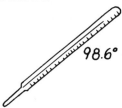

In warm-blooded animals (mammals) each species maintains a normal, average body temperature. The normal, average body temperature of the human being is 98.6° F.

Body heat is produced in each cell when digested food combines with oxygen in a burning process known as *oxidation*. This burning process makes it possible for us to have the energy (heat is an important form of energy) to use our muscles and to perform all of the body activities necessary to maintain life.

When you are ill, your temperature sometimes rises above 98.6° F. This indicates to the doctor that there may be an invasion of germs causing your illness. The "soldier cells" and "antibodies" in your blood hasten to try to fight and kill these unwelcome intruders. Extra body heat is produced because the blood is working overtime in an emergency battle to overcome the germs.

HOW THE SKIN THROWS OFF BODY WASTES

Follow this procedure: Observe the skin of your arm on a summer day after you have perspired. Rub your finger tip over it and taste lightly with the tip of your tongue.

You will observe: The skin will be moist with perspiration, what many of us call "sweat." This has a definite salty taste.

Like the lungs and the kidneys, the skin serves as a waste-collecting and waste-ridding organ of the body. Liquid wastes, including water, urea and excess salts, are brought to the skin by the circulating blood, which picked up these waste materials from the cells of the body.

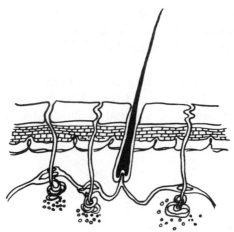

Certain glands in the lower layers of the skin extract these wastes from the blood. These are the sweat glands which collect waste products and send them to the surface of the skin through long tubes. The pores on the surface of your skin are the openings of the tubes, or *ducts*, of the sweat glands.

THE SKIN — A BUILT- IN THERMOSTAT

Materials: Cold water, rubbing alcohol, absorbent cotton.

Follow this procedure: Wet a piece of absorbent cotton with water and sponge the inside of your left wrist with it. How does your wrist feel as the water dries?

Immediately after, sponge your right wrist with another piece of absorbent cotton soaked in rubbing alcohol. How does your wrist feel after the alcohol has dried?

Which liquid dries more rapidly?

You will observe: The alcohol will dry more rapidly than the water.

Your left wrist will feel cool as the water dries, but your right wrist will feel even cooler.

As water evaporates (dries) from the surface of the skin, it removes a certain amount of body heat. Since alcohol evaporates faster than water, it cools the body faster than does water.

Your skin is a built-in thermostat. As perspiration, or sweat, evaporates from your skin some body heat is driven off, making the body generally cooler. Therefore, it is to your advantage to perspire in the summer.

Since bathing the skin with alcohol hastens the loss of heat, doctors recommend alcohol baths when a person is ill and has a high fever. An alcohol bath will lower a "fever" somewhat. A high temperature causes the heart to work much harder than usual, so it is important to keep body temperature as near normal as possible.

In the summer the use of cologne or toilet water (both of which have a high alcohol content) helps make you feel cooler.

STUDYING A LAMB KIDNEY

Materials: Get a pair of lamb kidneys at a butcher shop or supermarket. Ask the butcher to cut one of them in half the long way. If you prefer, you can do this yourself.

Follow this procedure: First examine the external structure. Then look closely at the internal structure of one of the two halves of the divided kidney.

You will observe: Lamb kidneys are kidney-bean shaped and dark red. In the middle area of each kidney are small coiled tubules that seem to empty into a funnel-like area. This leads into a tube extending from the inner side of each kidney.

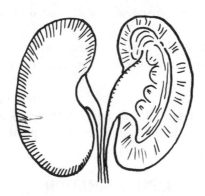

The lamb kidneys are similar in size and shape to those of human beings. Like lambs, we have a pair of kidneys located at the small of the back, one on each side of the backbone.

Blood carrying liquid wastes from all parts of the body passes through the kidneys where excess water and a large quantity of liquid waste are strained out and collected in the small tubules you observed. From these, waste matter passes into the funnel-like area of each kidney through tubes into the storage *bladder*.

The bladder stores liquid wastes, now called urine, until they are eliminated from the body.

THE STRENGTH OF HABIT

Materials: You need several companions for this exercise. In fact, it makes a lively game for a party. Provide each participant with pencil and paper.

Follow this procedure: Read the following sentences rapidly to your companions. Instruct them to write exactly what you read as fast as they can *without* crossing any t's or dotting any i's.

After you have finished, count up the number of t's crossed and the i's your companions have dotted.

These are the sentences:

Indians like kittens and little rabbits. They take tiny arrows to hunt these animals with.

The rain hit the window like soft tufts of cattails.

Time and tide wait for no man.

After tea for two the twins left the inn.

You will observe: Even though they were instructed not to do so, most of your companions will have crossed several t's and dotted several i's.

Dotting i's and crossing t's when writing is a deeply ingrained habit. A habit develops after you have repeated the same thing, in the same manner, over and over again.

Good habits are of great advantage to us. They save time and energy. They enable us to do certain things automatically so as to have time and energy to concentrate on things which require a great deal of thought and judgment.

HABIT FORMATION

Materials: Pencils and sheets of paper. Ask several friends to participate in this experiment. The more the merrier; this game would be a good one for a party.

Follow this procedure: Ask your companions to divide their sheets of paper into two columns headed A and B. Ask them to write their full names in Column A, as many times as they can in a minute. At the end of this time, ask them to write their full names backward in Column B as many times as they can. Again, call time at the end of a minute.

Count the number of times the name was written in each column.

You will observe: Very few names will appear in Column B.

When you were very young you learned to write the combination of letters that is your name, and ever since you have written it in much the same way. Writing your name has become a habit, a good habit that is time-saving because it is automatic.

Since writing a name backward is *not* a habit, your companions had a great deal of difficulty doing it quickly.

LEARNING BY TRIAL-AND-ERROR

Materials: A watch with a minute hand or a stop watch, several shirt cardboards, a ruler, a pencil, a pair of scissors. Although you can perform this experiment by yourself, it's more fun when there are several participants. Then it becomes a game.

Follow this procedure: Cut each cardboard in lengths measuring 2 x 4 inches. Mark each 2 x 4-inch rectangle as shown in the illustration below and cut each into four pieces as indicated.

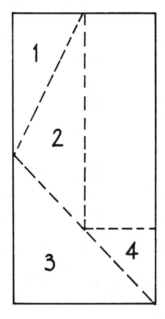

Scramble the four pieces you cut from each cardboard. At a given signal (marked by your watch), each person should arrange the scrambled pieces to form the letter L. Keep a record of each contestant's time.

As soon as each player has completed the letter L, have him rescramble the pieces and put them together again five times. This time, each player should keep his own record of the time required to make the letter L.

You will observe: The first time, it will take the longest to assemble the L. Each time thereafter it will take less time.

This is an example of the trial-and-error method of learning. Using this method you improve your ability to perform a given task by *repetition*. Babies learn by trial-and-error, as do many animals.

A SIMPLE LESSON IN "LEARNING"

Materials: Sharpened pencils and several sheets of paper. Again, you will want to include friends in this experiment.

Follow this procedure: Provide each person who is taking part with the following three lists of words (some "nonsense" and some "sense").

A	B	C
vip	shoe	grass
lor	tub	grows
tup	house	greener
joz	cat	where
nem	dish	the
hab	dog	soil
maf	tag	is
cas	school	rich

Ask your companions to read over List A silently three times. Then cover it with a piece of paper, and ask them to write the list of words on a new piece of paper in the correct order. Do the same for List B and then for List C. Have each person score his own paper by allowing one credit for each correct word (in its proper place).

You will observe: Scores will be poorest for List A. They will be better for List B, but List C will show the highest scores.

The "words" in List A are really not words at all, but nonsense syllables. They will be unfamiliar to your friends and, therefore, very difficult to remember.

The words in List B are all familiar but the order in which they are listed is not meaningful. Thus, they are easier to learn in proper order than the words in List A, but more difficult than the ones in List C.

The third list (List C) is really a sensible sentence. Its meaning ties the words together, making them relatively easy to remember even after the first reading. The scores for List C will be high; some may be perfect.

Learning in school or from reading a book involves the same processes. When you study a vocabulary list, the words will be easier to remember if you make up a sentence using the words.

When you read a paragraph in a book you may come across a word that is unfamiliar. You may be able to guess the meaning of the word from its relationship to the rest of the paragraph with which you are familiar.

INDEX